Peaceful Parenting Handbook

A Parent's Simple Strategy for Connecting with Their Children and Raising Happy Kids

Nora Williams

Uranus Publishing

Copyright © 2021 by Nora Williams

All rights reserved.

ISBN 978-1-915218-05-6

This book is copyright protected, and it is only for personal use. You cannot amend, distribute, sell, use, quote, or paraphrase any part of this book's content without the author or publisher's consent. All pictures contained in this book come from the author's archive or copyright-free stock websites.

Disclaimer Notice:

Please note the information contained within this document is for educational and entertainment purposes only. All effort has been executed to present accurate, up-to-date, reliable, complete information. No warranties of any kind are declared or implied. Readers acknowledge that the author is not engaged in rendering legal, financial, medical or professional advice. The content within this book has been derived from various sources. Please consult a licensed professional before attempting any techniques outlined in this book.

By reading this document, the reader agrees that under no circumstances is the author responsible for any losses, direct or indirect, that are incurred due to the use of the information contained within this document, including, but not limited to, errors, omissions, or inaccuracies.

The trademarks used are without any consent, and the publication of the trademark is without permission or backing by the trademark owner. All trademarks and brands within this book are for clarifying purposes only and are owned by the owners themselves, not affiliated with this document.

Contents

INTRODUCTION	1
1. PARENTING STYLES AND THEIR EFFECTS	5
2. MOST COMMON PARENTING MISTAKES	13
3. THE SECRET TO CALM PARENTING	37
4. THE PEACEFUL PARENTING APPROACH	61
5. SETTING BOUNDARIES	85
6. DEALING WITH TANTRUMS	103
7. UNDERSTANDING AND VALIDATING EMOTIONS	115
8. PEACEFULLY RESOLVING CONFLICTS	129
9. PARENTING THE ANXIOUS CHILD	139
10. PARENTING THE STRONG-WILLED	149

CHILD

11. MINDFULNESS IN PEACEFUL PARENTING   155

CONCLUSION   163

About Author   167

INTRODUCTION

Do you have a newborn at home and are contemplating parenting philosophies? Or if you already have children and are tired of constantly yelling at them? Or perhaps you've observed that all the yelling isn't truly changing behavior.

Here's a way you might want to try: calm parenting. It may sound like an oxymoron or a woo-woo philosophy involving holding hands and singing Kumbaya in the woods, but it's actually founded on research and is worth a look.

Most parents agree that one of the most crucial pillars of a happy and well-adjusted childhood is self-control. Without this foundation, children's emotional stability is easily shaken by peer provocation, criticism, and a slew of other "hard knocks" that aid in developing resilience in youngsters. However, some parents miss one of the essential components of laying this emotional and social foundation: parental self-control. When confronted with reactive children, reactive parents lose their cool instead of modeling appropriate restraint. Reactive parenting does not work when it comes to teaching self-control to a child.

But how does a reactive parenting style affect children's self-control?

Reactive parenting frequently has its origins in childhood. The daily challenges of parenting strain all parents' patience and sometimes "open windows" into one's own youth. If adults were raised with an authoritarian parenting style that included intimidation and terror, these techniques might be the only options when emotions flare. Instead of employing a parenting repertoire that emphasizes two-way communication between parent and kid, safety, and self-correction, the parent resorts to yelling and punishing. Those who acknowledge the negative impacts of harsh parenting on children are willing to try alternative approaches.

Identify your parenting hotspots so you can be ready for "rapid cooling." One method to forge a new parenting route is to consider what child behaviors set you off. This can involve noncompliance, sibling abuse, verbal/nonverbal contempt, or intentional disobedience. Accept that these behaviors are a natural part of everyone's parenting journey and not an excuse to become a hothead. Create a three-step plan to follow when a hotspot is detected: A for awareness, B for deep breathing, and C for responding calmly.

Strive to be a parent coach rather than a parent cop when responding. Parent cops use punishments and intimidation as their primary methods of discipline. Problem behaviors are considered as chances to assist children in self-correct when parents take on the coaching role. The game plan calls for asking children to express their point of view, express their understanding, describe the consequences of poor conduct, and offer alternatives. Remember that showing understanding is not the same as agreeing and that when presenting consequences, it is critical to underline the impact misbehavior has on trust, privileges, and pleasant surprises.

Use a calm tone of voice and language that encourage a two-way conversation. "Let's work out how we can both handle this problem without losing our cool" is one method to kick off a fruitful coaching huddle. This type of opening reduces the child's defensiveness. It paves the way for the parent to avoid the frequent mistakes of reactive parenting: accusing, blaming and controlling (the other ABCs to avoid).

Remember that most misbehavior is a message, and it is the parent's responsibility to decipher the meaning, so the communication is clearer and more acceptable. Stress the significance of communicating with the appropriate tone, words, and actions. Huddle with your child about the difficulties regularly, even if they aren't happening, to show them you haven't forgotten about their concerns and that you appreciate their development.

When you quit employing the reactive parenting style, your family life will calm down, and everyone will feel better after a time.

That's what this book is going to teach you. We'll take you through the child's brain and show you the best ways to teach them the right way to behave. We'll also dispel some myths and mistakes along the way not to fall into parenting traps. Let's begin!

Chapter One
PARENTING STYLES AND THEIR EFFECTS

Your parenting style can have a huge impact on anything, from your child's weight to how they think about themselves. It is essential to ensure that your parenting style promotes healthy growth since the way you connect with your child and punish them will affect them for the rest of their life. Researchers have found four types of parenting styles:

- Authoritarian
- Authoritative
- Permissive
- Uninvolved

Each parenting style has a unique approach to child-rearing and can be distinguished by a variety of traits.

Authoritarian parenting

Do any of these statements apply to you?

- You feel that children should be seen rather than heard.
- You believe that "my way or the highway" is the only way when it comes to rules.
- You are unconcerned with your child's sentiments.

If any of these statements apply to you, you may be an authoritarian parent. Authoritarian parents feel that their children must obey the rules without exception.

When a child asks the reasoning for a regulation, authoritarian parents are famous for replying, "Because I said so." They are not interested in bargaining and are just concerned with compliance.

They also do not permit children to participate in problem-solving challenges or barriers. Instead, they create the rules and execute the consequences with little regard for the opinions of children.

Punishments may be used instead of discipline by authoritarian parents. So, rather than teaching a youngster how to make better decisions, they are more interested in making children feel sorry for their failures.

Children raised by strict authoritarian parents tend to follow regulations the majority of the time. Their obedience, though, comes at a cost.

Children of authoritarian parents are more likely to suffer self-esteem issues because their opinions are not appreciated. They may become hostile or aggressive as well. Rather than considering how to do things better in the future, kids frequently focus on their feelings of resentment toward their parents. Because authoritarian parents are frequently severe, their children may grow up to be good liars in order to avoid punishment.

Authoritative parenting

Do any of these statements apply to you?

- You have worked hard to establish and maintain a positive relationship with your child.
- You explain why your rules are the way they are.

- You enforce rules and impose punishments while keeping your child's feelings in mind.

If you recognize such statements, you may be an authoritative parent. Authoritarian parents set rules and apply punishments, but they also consider their children's thoughts. They validate their children's emotions while simultaneously emphasizing that adults are ultimately in charge.

Authoritarian parents devote time and commitment to preventing behavioral issues before they occur. Positive discipline tactics, such as praise and reward systems, are also used to promote positive behavior.

According to studies, children who grow up with authoritative parents are more likely to become responsible people who feel comfortable expressing their thoughts. Children who are raised with strict discipline are more likely to be happy and successful. They're also more likely to be capable of making independent judgments and assessing safety threats.

Permissive parenting

Do any of these statements apply to you?

- You make rules but rarely follow them.
- You don't hand out punishments very often.
- You believe that allowing your children to learn on their own is the greatest way to learn.

If you recognize such statements, you may be a lenient parent. Permissive parents are forgiving, and they frequently only intervene when there is a significant problem. They're quite forgiving, with the idea that "kids will be kids." When they do apply consequences, they may not make them stay. They may restore privileges if the child pleads, or they may let a child out of time-out early if he/she agrees to be good.

Permissive parents frequently play the role of a friend rather than a parent. They frequently urge their children to talk to them about their issues, but they rarely make an attempt to discourage poor choices or bad behavior.

Children raised by permissive parents are more likely to suffer academically. They may exhibit greater behavioral issues since they do not value authority and regulations. They frequently have low self-esteem and may express a great deal of melancholy. They are also more likely to develop health problems, such as obesity, because permissive parents struggle to regulate junk food intake. They are significantly more likely to develop dental cavities since permissive parents rarely enforce positive behaviors, such as ensuring their children wash their teeth.

Uninvolved parenting

Do any of these statements ring a bell?

- You don't inquire about school or homework with your child.
- You rarely know where your children are or who they are with.
- You do not spend a lot of time with your child.

If those statements ring true for you, you may be an uninvolved parent. Uninvolved parents often have limited information about their children's activities. There aren't many rules, and children may not receive as much instruction, caring, or parental attention as they should.

Uninvolved parents expect their children to raise themselves, and they don't put much effort or time into satisfying the basic requirements of children. Uninvolved parents may be neglectful, but it is not always intentional. A parent who has a mental illness or substance misuse, for example, may be unable to meet a child's physical or emotional requirements consistently.

At times, uninvolved parents are unaware of their child's development. And sometimes, they're simply overburdened with other issues, such as employment, bills, and household management.

Children who have uninvolved parents are more prone to struggle with low self-esteem. They have a dismal academic record. They also have regular behavioral issues and are unsatisfied.

What is the best parenting style for you?

Sometimes parents may not fit into a single category, so don't be discouraged if you have periods or regions where you are lenient and others who are more authoritative. It isn't easy to maintain consistency while juggling life and parenthood. Don't be a victim of parental guilt or shame, that won't be helpful.

According to research, authoritative parents are more likely to raise autonomous, self-sufficient, and socially competent children. While children of authoritative parents are not immune to mental or interpersonal issues, substance misuse, poor self-regulation, or low self-esteem, these characteristics are more likely in children of parents who rigorously practice authoritarian, permissive, or uninvolved parenting styles.

Of course, there is no such thing as a "one-size-fits-all" approach to parenting. You don't have to subscribe to just one style because there may be occasions when you need to adopt various parenting methods - but only in moderation.

The most effective parents understand when to adapt their parenting approach to the circumstances. When a child is unwell, an authoritative parent, for example, may desire to become more permissive by continuing to offer warmth while relinquishing some control (e.g., "Sure, you can have some ice cream after lunch."). Likewise, when a child's safety is in danger, such as when crossing a busy street, a permissive parent may be more stringent (e.g., "You're going to hold my hand whether you like it or not.").

Finally, use your best judgment and keep in mind that the parenting style that works best for your family at the time is the one you should use.

Chapter Two
MOST COMMON PARENTING MISTAKES

We live in an increasingly stressful society, making it more vital than ever to instill emotional and mental resilience in our children. Not only are mentally strong children better prepared to deal with future challenges on their own, but studies have shown that they are also more likely to be engaged in school and in future employment.

Being a mother or father requires a delicate balance of caring for your children while also allowing them to mature and learn from their mistakes. Your responsibility as a parent shifts from merely loving and protecting your child from suffering and discomfort to understanding that they will need to face the natural consequences of their behavior.

The difficult part—both for them and for us—is that these repercussions may sometimes involve some discomfort, disappointment, and pain.

Hardest parenting challenges

Parents face numerous challenges. And, as we all discover, there are many issues that we did not expect before having children! As a mother and therapist, I've found the following five to be the most challenging.

<u>Parent the child you have, not the child you desire</u>

We frequently try to parent our children based on who we believe they should be rather than who they really are. Having a child with ADHD or an adolescent with ODD who is stubborn and ill-mannered can definitely be draining. You could also have a child who is very different from you. Trying to see things from their perspective becomes a never-ending, exhausting effort.

"Hey, this isn't what I signed up for!" you could think. Is this what it's like to be a mother?"

As a mother and therapist, I know that real grief may arise when you learn your child is not who you expected them to be. You may have to give up some dreams you had for your child's future if they do not follow the path you had hoped they would.

Understand, though, that once you let go and accept your child for who they are, a different sort of love can emerge. You'll be able to accept them for who they truly are.

True acceptance, I've discovered, is one of the most powerful and loving things a parent can give to their child. It serves as the foundation for many things, including setting and conveying realistic expectations for appropriate behavior. Old power battles dissolve, allowing you to cultivate new areas of your partnership. As an added plus, when you embrace your child for who they are, they can learn to accept themselves.

Allow your child to feel the hurt of natural consequences

In general, attempting to shield your child from the repercussions of their conduct is a bad idea. How will your child learn from their poor choices if the natural repercussions of those choices are removed?

Trial and error are how we humans learn, and it is frequently the most effective method of learning. We speed, get a ticket, and then we stop speeding. If you put up a protective fence around your child and try to fix things, they will not learn this way. Change occurs as a result of struggle and when we accept responsibility for our actions.

It is our responsibility as parents to help our children get through difficult times, but it is not our responsibility to shoulder all of their responsibilities for them. This may imply allowing your child to experience sorrow and disappointment.

You can assist them by discussing how they can conduct themselves differently the next time and teaching them some effective coping skills. Simply letting your child know you're there for them because you truly love them is one of the most meaningful and beautiful gifts a parent can give to their child.

Dealing with judgment, shame, and blame from others

If you have a child that acts out and engages in other problem behaviors—tantrums, yelling, defying you, or being annoying and obnoxious—you've probably received "the look" from both friends and strangers. You know the one: "What's wrong with you?" "Why aren't you doing anything about your child's bad behavior?"

Even if you know you're doing everything you can to raise your child the best way possible, the look that others give you can make you feel like a bad parent. And the truth is that other people will certainly judge you— it's human nature.

It's reasonable to be concerned about your child disappointing or embarrassing you in this situation. It's also reasonable to be concerned about how others may react to your child's misbehavior and point the finger at you. However, if your child is misbehaving and you are feeling criticized by others, pause and tell yourself:

"I can't read other people's minds."

Indeed, if you try to imagine what others are thinking, you will almost always read something bad. This is because when we are negative, we interpret other people's impressions of us as negative as well. And in these cases, we don't read people's brains to find hope. We read them to find criticism, especially when things go wrong.

So, the next time you find yourself attempting to guess what your neighbor, sister-in-law, or friends are thinking, tell yourself:

"I'm not a mind reader, and I have no idea what they're thinking."

Stop listening to the recording in your head and go on. This is also part of learning how to engage in "positive self-talk," or talking to yourself in a way that fosters calm and hope rather than panic and frustration.

Accept when your child says, "I hate you, Mom!"

One of the most difficult situations for parents is when their child is harsh, impolite, or disrespectful. Your child may have always been this way. Or the change in their personality may have appeared to develop overnight, perhaps when they reached their adolescent years. One day, your 10-year-old enjoys spending time with you. The next day, they're yelling, "I hate you," calling you names and refusing to accompany you anyplace.

Any parent can be moved to tears or enraged by the words "I hate you" from their child. It can make you feel like you've failed and leave you wondering what went wrong. Kids understand that repeating these words can paralyze a parent during a quarrel, so they employ this approach to achieve what they want. Especially if it's difficult, try not to personalize your child's conduct, even if they declare they despise you. Personalization makes it difficult to be impartial about how to respond to your child at the moment. When this happens, it's a good idea to pause, take a deep breath, and answer with something like this:

"We're not going to get into that right now. I'm referring to the fact that you must complete your homework."

You can also ask yourself the following questions:

"What does my child need right now?"

It could be some extra space, and it could also be for you to carry out a consequence you issued. But remember not to take your children's statements personally.

<u>Say goodbye</u>

You are continuously presented with the problem of letting go during your child's pre-adolescent and adolescent years. This is especially challenging if your child appears to need to learn things the hard way. Risk-taking is a normal element of adolescence, and it frequently leads to rule-breaking and inappropriate behavior. It is critical for you as a parent to be able to disengage from your emotional reaction to this misbehavior.

Feelings of guilt, embarrassment, shame, or disappointment are examples of emotional responses. When our children reach a certain age, we as parents must step back and become coaches and teachers, allowing them to begin to play the game of life. We still love our children as persons, but we need to give them some space to grow and experiment.

Our children are born to move away from us, as difficult as it may be to accept at times. A sensation of bereavement accompanies this, and I've had firsthand experience with it. It's crucial to realize that caring for our children as they continually grow apart from us and become individuals can be stressful, demanding, and perplexing.

It might be tough for parents to determine what is correct. And the truth is that there isn't always a correct answer. Accept that there are choices to be made and that those decisions are frequently fraught with tension.

Remember that you are doing your best and that you will not be flawless. Being a "good enough" parent is more important than aiming to be a "perfect" parent. A "good enough" parent looks after their child and gives their all.

Life is full of difficult situations. However, these situations can help us learn and grow. You must accept the fact that you cannot shield your children from everything that could go wrong or from terrible decisions they may make. However, you may assist kids in learning from the negative situations they find themselves in. Your child will most likely not thank you now for allowing them to struggle on their own and suffer as a result, but when they're an adult, they may surprise you by saying that your coaching, teaching, or restriction set had a good influence on their life.

Harmful mistakes most parents make

It might be somehow difficult for parents to avoid these mistakes, but if you want your children to grow mentally and physically healthy, it's crucial to stay away from the following fatal errors:

<u>Minimizing your child's emotions</u>

Children must understand that expressing and discussing their feelings is healthy. When parents tell their children things like "don't be so upset about it" or "it's not a big deal, come on, you shouldn't be angry," they deliver the message that feelings are unimportant and that it is preferable to conceal them.

Consider this statement instead, "I know you're terrified right now," if your child is showing signs of dread during a noisy storm. Then inquire as to what they believe might help them feel better. This teaches children how to deal with and manage their emotions on their own.

The idea is to assist them in thinking about solutions until they find something that works for them.

Always saving them from failure

It's difficult for us as parents to watch our children struggle with problems that we know we can easily solve for them.

But consider this: if your child is struggling in school, you know that telling them the homework answers will only backfire because you won't be able to be present in the classroom when they have to finish those tests on their own.

Failure is an essential component of success. If children are never allowed to learn the lessons of failure, they will never develop the perseverance required to recover from a difficult situation.

Indulging your children excessively

Kids enjoy receiving gifts, and parents enjoy rewarding their kids. However, research suggests that when you give your children whatever they want, they miss out on mental strength abilities like self-discipline.

You want your children to grow up thinking that anything is possible if they work hard enough. Parents can teach self-control to their children by establishing clear rules for things like finishing homework before watching television or doing chores to increase allowance (so they can buy things on their own while knowing they earned it).

Demanding excellence

It's natural to want your child to strive for greatness and excel at everything. That, however, is not how things work. Setting the bar too high might lead to challenges with self-esteem and confidence later in life.

Create mental strength in your children by setting reasonable expectations. Even if your children do not meet them, the challenges they confront will teach them essential life skills and how to succeed the next time.

Ensuring that they are constantly at ease

Many activities can make your child feel uneasy, especially if they are doing something new, such as trying new foods, making new friends, participating in a new sport, or moving houses and attending a new school.

Embracing uncomfortable circumstances, including failure, can increase mental power. Encourage your children to experiment with new things. Assist them in getting started, as this is the most challenging phase. However, after they take that first step, they may discover that it isn't as difficult as they imagined it would be – and that they may even be brilliant at it!

Failure to establish parental-child boundaries

You want your children to be able to make their own decisions, but they also need to know who is in charge. For example, if you give your 12-year-old a curfew, make sure they follow it every night (or as much as possible).

Mentally strong children have parents who appreciate the value of boundaries and consistency. When you cave in and allow rules to be negotiated too frequently, it can lead to power battles between you and your child.

Not taking care of yourself

The more we get older, the more difficult it is to maintain good behaviors (e.g., eating healthy, exercising daily, taking time to restore). That is why it is critical to model self-care habits for your children.

It's also important to demonstrate healthy coping strategies in front of your children. If you're stressed about work, for example, you can tell your child, "I had a really long day at work, and I'm going to relax with a hot coffee and a good book."

Six Ineffective Parenting Roles

Let's face it: we're all imperfect parents in some way. Even though no one gets it right all of the time, it's still easy to criticize and call oneself a "good parent" or "poor parent" based on how you handle a specific scenario. It is important to be a 'good enough parent." A good enough parent watches after their child, does their best and seeks assistance when necessary. The good news is that you can work on improving your child's conduct by becoming a more effective parent.

Identifying your own parenting style to see what works and what doesn't is one of the fundamental building blocks of mindful parenting. A parenting style, sometimes known as a "role," is how you respond to parenting situations regularly. If you see that your child's behavior isn't changing (or is getting worse), taking a step back and taking a closer look might be quite beneficial. As the saying goes, "insanity is doing the same thing over and over and expecting different results." By understanding your role as a parent, you can learn how to do things differently to influence your child's behavior.

Here are six basic roles that parents frequently find themselves in—and how to break free from them.

<u>The Master Negotiator</u>

Many of us can connect with this inadequate parenting technique. You may be an over-negotiator if you enable your child to negotiate consequences, boundaries, and rules, often succeeding in getting you to distort the rules in their favor. These parents may consent to a lenient punishment after an inappropriate behavior simply because their child talks them into it. Because he knows boundaries can be modified at any time, your youngster becomes adept at pushing them. If you have this unsuccessful parenting style, you're undoubtedly used to fights and debates over the fairness of the rules and whether or not your expectations are reasonable.

The remedy is for the over-negotiating parent to be strong in their rules, expectations, and punishments. Allow your child to amend the rules or negotiate a different punishment after the fact. You can assist your child in becoming accountable for their behavior by remaining firm and unambiguous.

The Screamer

The parent who screams and yells at their child is frequently behaving out of profound irritation and tiredness. While this is natural (most parents have been there), it is unlikely that losing your anger will result in positive behavioral improvements in your child. If you engage in screaming battles, name-calling, or threatening your child, you convey the message that you are not in control. This also implies that your authority is in jeopardy. It's as if you've descended to your child's behavioral level for that brief instant. The mom or dad caught in this unsuccessful parenting approach may even be dragged into justifying their behavior; their child can easily divert their behavior difficulties by pointing out how terribly their parent is behaving.

The solution: The screamer parent needs to learn more effective ways to deal with their displeasure and aggravation. We all get tired (or worked up) and snap from time to time, and it comes with the territory of parenthood. However, unless you learn to control and manage your temper, your child is unlikely to regard you as the calm, clear authority that they require.

The Martyr

This parent never wants to watch their child struggle or suffer. If you wish to shield your child from painful emotions, you may strive relentlessly to ensure that they do not feel excluded or frustrated. You can find yourself working far harder than your youngster on homework or projects. You want your child's journey to be as easy as possible. How can this be a bad thing?

The truth is, when you rush in to do things for your child, you're actually giving the message that you don't believe they'll be able to handle the situation successfully on their own. That could be correct! You might be concerned that they won't be able to pull it off. However, you must know that children gain problem-solving skills as they fail. They can only learn to deal with frustration if they are exposed to it. You are preventing your child from understanding their power if you make the road too easy for them, sheltering them from every possibility of failure or frustration. Plus that, you're wearing yourself out in the process!

The remedy for the martyr parent is to cease working so hard. Instead of wearing yourself out, allow your child to experience sadness or frustration. The most beneficial thing you can do is to only assist them in coping with their emotions. When in doubt, ask yourself, "Am I doing something that my child can accomplish for themselves?" and the situation will be more clear for you to act.

The Overachiever

The perfectionist parent is the polar opposite of the martyr: instead of seeing everything your child achieves as fantastic, this parent sees everything they do as inadequate. Parents who are locked in this unsuccessful parenting style recognize that their children have outstanding talents; they just need to work harder to develop them. So, what makes that ineffective? The fact that perfectionist parent instills in their child that failure is NOT to be expected. Why should a youngster even try if they will never be able to meet their parents' very high expectations? If the child succeeds, the perfectionist parent will frequently increase the bar, believing that their child can do even better the next time.

Perfectionist parents frequently believe they know their child so well that they know exactly what they're thinking. They frequently presume the worst, recognizing their child's assumed negative attitude before the child ever speaks their tongue. What makes this ineffective? Unfortunately, you're teaching your child not to display their feelings, to keep their accomplishments to themselves, and to avoid engaging with you. Why? Because they are aware that they will never be good enough. You're not educating your child to achieve their full potential; instead, you're teaching them to tremble at every correction.

The remedy is for the perfectionist parent to put some distance between themselves and their child—at the very least, between their expectations and their child's actual interests. Negative reinforcement, shouting, and hypercriticism will not help children improve. Encouraging your child to achieve their goals and discover their inherent skills creates a far better environment for growth.

<u>Bottomless Pockets</u>

The parent with boundless pockets wishes to connect with their child by providing them whatever they desire. We see this a lot in households where the child spends time with two sets of parents/stepparents, but it can also happen within the same household. The bottomless pockets parent, often known as the "over-giver," frequently lavishes material gifts on their children to alleviate or prevent behavioral issues. It's sometimes easier for the parent to spend money - even if it's money they don't have – than dealing with their child's reactions when they hear 'no.'

This instills a false attitude of entitlement in your child, and they know how to trick you into giving them what they desire. Since material goods are easily obtained, the child is not exposed to the reality of needing to work for the rewards or compensation. This can prepare children not only for future issues in the adult workplace but also for defining and accomplishing personal goals.

The solution is for the parent with unlimited funds to learn to say no—and to tolerate their child's outbursts when they don't receive what they want. If you want to utilize material objects as a reward for your child, make sure they are tied to tangible expectations, effort, and accomplishments rather than simply because they requested.

The Ticket-Puncher

The parent trapped in this ineffectual role acts as their child's best friend, going above and beyond to understand their child's wants and motivations, frequently identifying quite strongly with their child.

For instance, if you disliked school as a youngster, you may belittle or minimize your child's terrible school behavior, and after all, you're aware of what he's going through. In most cases, the ticket puncher parent stands with the child, joining them in badmouthing authority figures or disobeying rules they feel irrelevant.

The issue with this parenting method is not that you understand your child but that you let your understanding prohibit you from obeying the rules. The following case scenario has probably repeated itself in the history of human beings a million times: suppose your child can persuade you that their arguments are valid, you are finally convinced, and therefore they won't sense the need to change their behavior. As a result, you may blame others for your child's negative influence rather than seeing your child as solely responsible for their bad behavior.

The solution for the ticket-punching parent is to draw a clear line between understanding their child and making them responsible for their behavior. Just because you understand your child's frustration does not excuse them from following the rules; remember that you can be empathetic while simultaneously stating your expectations about their actions.

Parenting is a complex task, and examining your patterns and behaviors can be hard as well. Consider this while reflecting on your parenting style: it's never a question of whether your style is right or wrong, but of whether it's currently working to generate the behavior you want to see in your child. The bottom line is that poor parenting skills do not foster transformation or accountability in children. To effectively help your child grow and evolve, you must parent in ways that encourage growth and change.

Signs you are too strict with your child

Do you ever question if you're too hard on your child? Do you have concerns that your expectations are too high? Do you ever wonder if the punishments you impose on your child are a little too severe? Here are 15 indicators that you are too severe with your child.

<u>You have a strict no-tolerance policy</u>

While it is critical to have clear norms, it is also critical to acknowledge that there are always exceptions to the rules. Instead of taking an authoritative attitude on everything, demonstrate a readiness to analyze your child's behavior in the context of the situation.

<u>Your child tells a lot of lies</u>

While it is common for children to stretch the truth from time to time, research shows that harsh discipline develops children into good liars. If you are too harsh, your child will most likely lie to avoid punishment.

Your child is subjected to more restrictions than other children

There's nothing wrong with having rules that differ from the other parents'. However, if you're consistently the most rigorous parent in the room, it could be an indication that your expectations are too high.

You're not a patient person when it comes to silliness

Most children enjoy crazy jokes and stupid activities. While those jokes can become old quickly and goofy behavior can slow you down, it's crucial to enjoy the moment and have fun every now and then.

You are troubled by other people's lack of discipline

Strict parents frequently find it difficult to tolerate everything, from how a teacher runs a school to how Grandma addresses the child's problem behavior. It is okay for children to be exposed to adults who have diverse rules and methods of discipline.

You have loads of rules

Rules are needed, but too many rules can be detrimental. Maintain a simple set of rules and include the most critical ones you want your youngster to remember. Post your list of household rules somewhere you'll be able to refer to it when you need to.

Your child doesn't have enough time to have fun

Many children with strict parents rush from one activity to the next with little time to rest. While the structure is necessary, it is also crucial for children to have free time.

You make no provision for natural consequences

Strict parents may frequently go to tremendous efforts to prevent their child from making a mistake. However, when children confront natural consequences, they are generally capable of learning from their mistakes.

You have a lot of nagging

Nagging hinders children from accepting responsibility for their own actions. If you constantly nag your child about everything, from when to do their homework to practicing the violin, they will never learn to accomplish those things independently.

You are constantly giving out directions

Your youngster will tune you out if you constantly repeat things like, "Sit up straight," "Quit dragging your feet," and "Don't gulp your drink." If you want that your voice gets heard, save your instructions for essential subjects.

You do not provide options

Instead of asking, "Would you prefer to put your clothes away first or make your bed?" harsh parents frequently yell instructions. Giving your child a little leeway, especially when both options are positive, can go a long way toward securing their obedience.

You don't let your children do things their way

Sometimes stern parents demand that their children do things a certain way. They are adamant about making the bed "properly" or playing with the dollhouse "appropriately." While children do require adult supervision at times, it is also crucial to allow them flexibility and creativity.

You reward the result rather than the effort

Strict parents don't usually lavish praise on their children, and they save their affirmations for excellence rather than effort. If you only congratulate your child for achieving a perfect score on an exam or scoring more goals in a game, they may believe that your affection is conditional on an outstanding achievement.

You make heinous threats

While most parents are guilty of issuing an exaggerated threat now and then, strict parents make exaggerated threats regularly. They frequently say things like, "Clean up your room right now, or I'm going to toss all your toys in the garbage!" Avoid making threats that you aren't willing to follow through on, and make sure the repercussions are aimed at disciplining rather than punishing your child.

The emphasis is always on learning.

Strict parents frequently make every activity into a required lesson of some type. Children cannot color a picture unless they are challenged on their color knowledge. They cannot play with a dollhouse unless they are continually reminded of proper furniture arrangements. Playing, in and of itself, allows for imagination and creativity, and it may be a fun break from the typical structure and routine.

Chapter Three
THE SECRET TO CALM PARENTING

C alm is an internal sense of peace that allows us to function to the best of our abilities. It is the optimal state of the brain, backed by a body that is entirely associated with it, allowing us to harness our cognitive powers while maintaining emotional balance. You are in your zone when you are tranquil, unaffected by distractions or distress.

In order to counteract its mechanisms for alertness and worry, the brain includes intricate systems for relaxation and tranquility. These visceral systems are located within our core brain, which governs our emotions and impulses and the huge environmental sensor and receptacle that is our body, rather than our frontal lobes, our logical higher brain, the seat of logic and thinking.

A tranquil body leads to a quiet mind. Contrary to popular belief, it is not the other way around. When a mother asks her kid, "Harry, would you please calm down?" she utilizes a top-down method to calm her child, urging him to utilize a rational, conscious process to calm down. In contrast, if a mother tells a screaming child, "Time out!" and places him in a chair facing a wall, she utilizes a bottom-up approach—quieting his body to generate a sense of serenity.

Structure vs. Choice

I recently saw a lady with her little boy, who appeared to be about five years old, in a café. On a hectic Sunday morning, they strolled in and spotted a corner table set for four people.

"Where do you want to sit, honey?" the mother said, pointing to the four available seats.

"I'm not sure, Mom. "Wherever," the boy said, his voice still heavy with sleep.

"You have the option of sitting against the wall or in the corner. Or you can sit next to Mommy, right here," his mother replied, ignoring his apathy. "You can observe people arrive and depart if you sit next to the wall. What do you want to do?"

"I don't care, Mom," the son responded, starting to wail.

"OK, but don't cry about it afterward," the mother cautioned.

"Didn't you want to use your crayons to draw?"

"OK, OK. Here?" The son motioned to the corner seat.

"Good," his mother remarked, glad that he had made a choice. "What do you want for breakfast?"

That's how it went. This five-year-old had had to make so many judgments by the time they left the café. This is how the scene continued: he was fatigued. He used to think his mother was too strict, but after watching a tragic Sunday morning drama, he was pleased she put a plate in front of him every morning and made sure he ate what was on it.

Anxiety and overscheduling

There are too many toys, too much technology, and too many options in the increasingly overstimulated environment where modern children live. Community is one thing that youngsters, in my opinion, do not have enough of, and this is what the core brain necessitates. Children require the abilities learned from community living to help them empathize and communicate well, especially crucial for calm.

Overscheduling children's life in the race to Harvard, which begins at conception, leaves little time for impromptu recreation with neighborhood kids and other core-brain delights that give rise to peace and productive and healthy adulthood. In fact, researchers have discovered that the more scheduled activities children have, the more likely they are to suffer from stress and anxiety.

The ongoing requirement for alertness goes hand in hand with hectic scheduling. My patient informed me about her ten-year-old granddaughter, who lives in an apartment complex in New York City. Although the building has a doorman who keeps an eye on all visitors, it is not uncommon for parents to keep an eye on their child as they walk down the hall to visit another child's apartment. What dangers might be lurking in the corridor? This kind of fear about unknown hazards has to affect young children's impressionable core brains.

Whispered fears

Even at the hands of well-meaning parents, a childhood spent in constant vigilance might impair one's ability to self-soothe and self-protect. A few weeks ago, while walking along Madison Avenue in New York, I overheard a woman tell her three-year-old son, who was reclining in his stroller, "Aaron, close your eyes, it's getting sunny!" And young Aaron meekly closed his eyes to protect himself from a beautifully sunny day because his mother feared it would damage him.

This scenario is amusing in its silliness, but many children today are unsuspecting victims of their parents' germophobia and over-sanitization—of children and childhood. The truth is that early exposure to a reasonable number of environmental pathogens aids in developing immunity to a variety of illnesses in adulthood. Preventing this exposure can set the stage for eventual sickness susceptibility. On the other hand, overprotection can amplify those unidentified, unspoken worries that reverberate throughout the house, whispering into a child's ear, "Be scared!"

The expansion of technology, which is related to over-vigilance and a loss of community, further impedes children's quest for peace. Computer games jeopardize community and basic brain calm even further with their blaring and flashing and demands for intense technological focus. As does children's continuous texting, which interferes with the development of key cognitive skills. "I don't know if she likes me in real life!" stated a boy who flirts with a girl he adores through texting.

I make no claims to be an expert on children, and only my daughter can attest to how calm I am as a mother. However, it appears that understanding the neurology of a child's brain will assist parents in raising peaceful youngsters. Chess and piano classes are both excellent.

The best gift, though, is a quiet mind.

The parent-child relationship

Let's face it: in the child-parent connection, there is one adult with mature self-control and one youngster with significantly less self-control.

As a result, we, as parents, must regulate ourselves and assist our children in regulating.

Children are still uncivilized, unaware of or oblivious to the social conventions that govern when and how we express our emotions. It turns out that teaching our children how to express themselves in a way that recognizes their emotions while still being prosocial is one of our primary responsibilities as parents.

Early childhood is ideal for developing emotional and self-regulation skills since the brain is fully malleable and ready to learn. However, this also implies that it is immature, poorly connected in those places, and disorganized. It will be a long time before our efforts in teaching self-control to kids pay off. Depending on their age, temperament, and what is going on in their lives, our children are not yet well-equipped to deal with disappointment and frustration, to be able to calm down, focus on a goal, evaluate possibilities, or make well-considered decisions.

But how prepared are we as parents? What have we done in our lives to prepare ourselves for the arrival of a human being with limited self-control? Have you ever thought about these fundamental questions? Many people believe you can never be truly prepared for having a child. You have no idea of what it's like to be entirely responsible for someone else's life, to always be thinking of them, and to put their needs before your own prior to being a parent.

On the other hand, we've been preparing for this moment our entire lives — our childhood and adult experiences heavily influenced our self-regulation system. Some of us are better regulated by nature, while others may be better regulated by experience, but once the baby is born, we will all need to work on ourselves and adjust. After that, we'll have to keep adapting. As our children grow, so will we; however, our growth will be on the inside.

As parents, we frequently appear to have an instinct for knowing what our children require, but we often find ourselves perplexed, frustrated, and occasionally at odds with these little beings who have yet to learn the rules and methods of society. Take, for example, cutting a slice of toast or a sandwich into squares when triangles are intended! We talk a lot about how important it is to teach children self-regulation, but what about our own? How should we refine these abilities? How should I educate my son to manage his frustration when I can't manage mine?

Fortunately, our children have an uncanny ability to pinpoint exactly what we need to improve - they can push our buttons like no other! Our children, like Jedi Masters, will rapidly expose our flaws and test us daily. We simply have to accept the challenge and keep it in mind.

Five steps to being a calm and centered parent

Change your expectations and just observe

This, like everything else on this list, isn't something you do once and then forget about. Partly because your child is constantly changing and growing, your expectations of them will also alter.

I am guilty of placing much too high expectations on my son. It's simple – he's tall for his age and extremely vocal. I have to tell myself all the time that he's a child, and it's normal for him to be impetuous and overexcited. I have to remind myself (as have my son's instructors) that his physical and cognitive development does not correspond to his social and emotional development. That's fine; in fact, it's developmentally appropriate. Whatever stage of development your child is in is simply where they are.

As parents, we absolutely aid in their development, but we must also accept who they are. Children are likely to be more emotional than adults, and they are destined to have poor days with limited regulating abilities and constant cognitive jumps.

Remind yourself that self-control skills do not develop until the age of three and do not mature until the age of five or six. Continuous development occurs throughout childhood, followed by a second large growth surge in self-control in the brain during adolescence. According to some estimations, final maturation occurs at the age of thirty.

So, how do we reframe things?

When your child shouts because you sliced the toast incorrectly, rants because they can't build the Lego construction right, has a meltdown after school, or begins swirling around in a ball of emotions for no apparent reason, just stare at them and observe. Examine them as if they were from another planet because they are. Remember that their brains aren't yet as developed as ours. Consider their tininess. Observe them with open eyes and a keen sense of observation. You'll begin to identify with this little being who can't reason like an adult if you truly look at them.

Distancing your emotions from theirs

My graduate school acquaintance once told me about her approach to her son's meltdowns. Her words of wisdom have stayed with me for over ten years (and her kid is now grown and in college!).

"Just because he's having a breakdown doesn't mean I have to," she explained. His emotional management is independent of mine. I keep my cool since I'm not the one who is upset that gym playtime is over - he is."

It appears to be simple, but it is profound. It's also difficult to accomplish. When our children act out, we experience a stress response that can be exacerbated if it occurs in public. This is true for me, yet there have also been moments when I have remained calm. I just responded to their needs rather than reacting to them, and I kept my emotions under control. It's so much easier when I do that. It will be easier to assist them in coping and going on to the next item unhindered.

There is strength in remaining quiet. "How did you feel the last time you stayed calm?" I asked in a recent reader survey. Some of your responses are as follows:

"There's a lot of freedom for me in being calm while my daughter (or even the world around me) is feeling nothing but peace." I don't have to respond to everything. Instead, I may focus on the matter at hand and give it my all."

"I felt more in command of the situation, less apprehensive, and more confident." Because of my calm demeanor, I believe he responded better."

"I felt strong. I was able to fully relate and support myself without having to deal with my feelings. That doesn't always happen, but it would be lovely if it did."

How are you able to do this? It's a process, just like the others. But, with step one, you've already begun to control your own emotions by altering your expectations. The next stage is to figure out what your triggers are. "Self-monitoring" is frequently one of the first steps toward developing parental self-regulation.

Begin making a list of your triggers. What irritates you? It's noise for me; the louder it is, the more difficult it is for me to remain calm. And also, when other people are impacted, so I start worrying when we're out in public. I must brace myself for my son's emotions at these times — I must concentrate on myself.

How to find your center

When you notice yourself reacting, have a mantra ready (which has been demonstrated in imaging studies to relax the brain) – take a breath (a proven strategy to stop the stress response) and recite a simple sentence to yourself. Something that keeps you steady or calms you down. Here are several examples:

"Mama, Ride This Wave"

"Let It Be"

"I am their mother."

"I am here to help you."

It is beneficial to physically ground or center yourself while doing this, in my opinion. Engage your core (which has a calming effect on the body) and put your feet firmly on the ground, open and facing your child. Take a deep breath and repeat to yourself your mantra. You are now in a position of strength to weather their storm.

Create a parenting toolbox

How you address your child's regulation issues is connected with your own. You will feel more prepared if you have a plan for dealing with these scenarios. You will be better regulated if you feel more prepared.

You're also assisting kids in learning to self-regulate, right? I believe that our ability to educate our children about regulating themselves is inextricably linked to our own ability to regulate ourselves. The two systems must be linked in our brains, and I know our children will be unable to control if we are unable to do so.

My sister was the first to mention the phrase "my parenting toolbox" to me. She discussed how she felt more capable of dealing with emotional meltdowns or issues when she had solutions in her back pocket. She, like myself, is always on the lookout for new "tools."

You will be more effective in helping your child if you are regulated and respond to them rather than react to them. The next step is to assess your parental self-efficacy, or how confident you are in your capacity to influence your child's behavior and development. I know that having a strategy and having intentions for responding to my child makes me feel more confident.

Here's another option for getting started. Identify a trigger or stressful event - lately, our morning routines have been unpleasant, and I'm running out of patience. I began by attempting to determine the source of my stress. My son was waking up later and later, and we were running out of time. He was also less concentrated. As a result, I began waking my son up a little earlier, which also meant ensuring that he went to bed on time. I also made and printed a morning routine chart to assist him in staying on track.

Having a plan made me more intentional, rather than simply reacting to the event, and better able to remain calm.

Take care of yourself

Many of you responded that being well-rested was a key element in being able to keep calm in my last reader survey. Being well-rested and ready to confront obstacles is definitely our most difficult modern parenting task.

Perhaps it is difficult because we are too busy in this modern era. In addition, it's not beneficial at all, neither for ourselves nor for our children, that we are overtired, overspent, and just overdone. When I asked how you felt after a moment when you were able to keep calm with your child, you responded the following:

"It felt fantastic. I was still exhausted afterward, and honestly, I was concerned that the parenting responsibilities would just become more difficult."

"Even if I appeared to be calm on the outside, I felt like it was still emotionally stressful for me. It took me a few moments to settle down. Even though I had kept my cool on the outside."

"It was still a stressful situation for me. It seemed like it took a lot of effort to be calm. It was simpler to reconnect and help my child through the difficulty after the breakdown."

These responses are quite perceptive. Yes, we may feel empowered, but remaining calm has its costs. It's more difficult when we're fatigued or worried. We only have so much emotional capacity. When we notice our emotional supply diminishing, we must take the time to care for ourselves.

Part of that is admitting defeat and giving up on trying to do it all. And taking breaks when we need them. I must say that I'm still a work in progress on this one (even when I do take a break, I feel awful about it)! Amanda Rue offers some fantastic practical suggestions on how to take a break, even if you're at home with the kids and they're crazy!

The first step of the solution is being able to live in the present moment. Finding delight in the ordinary and in your daily routine will bring you up. It's both simple and difficult to do with children. On the one hand, when I stop trying and just be with them, they take me to a lovely world. On the other hand, children are repetitive, unregulated, and demanding. So, perspective plays a crucial role.

Understand what to do If you drop It

Because you will — I have, and you have, we can all agree on that. We've lost it in the most heinous ways on the most heinous days, and we've lost it when there was no need to, and we've lost it when it was the last straw.

But wouldn't it be strange if you never lost it? As a child, that would be something to strive for – perfect regulation at all times. Losing it is a natural aspect of life and relationships. Your children should see this, and they will. So, be kind to yourself and use this as an opportunity to teach your children about self-regulation:

- Own it – Admit to yourself that you lost your temper or became frustrated.
- Apologize – Parents make errors as well.
- Identify — Tell your youngster what you did to relax.

"I did become angry. Parents can get irritated as well. Everyone has emotions." "I yelled at you, which I should not have done." "I'm sorry if I offended you. But then I took a few deep breaths and relaxed, didn't

I?" "I adore you, and I will try not to lose my cool anymore."

Self-regulation is fantastic on so many levels: it demonstrates that everyone makes mistakes but that those mistakes can be overcome. It encourages your child to practice forgiveness and empathy. It teaches you how to self-regulate and make you aware of your weaknesses or trigger points. It also makes you aware of your own coping mechanisms or talents, allowing you to recommend them to your child when they are distressed. Finally, self-regulation assists your youngster in developing good relationship skills.

Just keep in mind that this is a journey, not a destination and that we are all on it together as parents. So, if you see a mother calmly handling his son's meltdown in the preschool parking lot, applaud her, and if you see her stressed and frantic, empathize with her.

How to calm yourself down

We're all worried and agitated from time to time, and that's totally normal. But what if your worry or fury takes over and you can't calm down? It is usually easier said than done to be able to relax in the heat of the moment.

That's why having a few tried-and-true tactics on hand can help you when you're feeling nervous or furious. Here are some useful, actionable things to try the next time you need to relax.

Breathe

Breathing is the most important and effective strategy for instantly lowering anger and anxiety.

When you're stressed or furious, you tend to take short, shallow breaths. It sends a message to your brain, resulting in a positive feedback loop reinforcing your fight-or-flight reaction. That's why taking long, deep, relaxing breaths breaks the loop and allows you to relax.

There are several breathing exercises that might help you relax. The first is three-part breathing, and it consists of taking one deep breath in and then thoroughly exhaling while paying attention to your body. Once you're comfortable with deep breathing, you can change the inhalation/expiration ratio to 1:2 (slow down your exhalation, so it's twice as long as your inhalation).

Practice these strategies when you're calm so you'll know what to do when you're nervous.

Admit that you are worried or angry

Allow yourself to express your anxiety or anger. When you define how you're feeling and allow yourself to express it, your worry and anger will most probably subside.

Examine your assumptions

Having irrational ideas that don't necessarily make sense is part of being distressed or furious. These are often "worst-case scenario" thinking. You may become trapped in the "what if" cycle, which can drive you to destroy many aspects of your life.

When you have one of these thoughts, come to a halt and ask yourself the following questions:

- Is this something that is likely to happen?
- Is this a reasonable idea?
- Is this anything that has happened to me before?
- What could possibly go wrong? Is it something I can handle?

After you've finished answering the questions, it's time to reframe your thinking. Instead of saying, "I can't walk across that bridge," say: "I can walk across that bridge." Instead of "What if there's an earthquake and it collapses into the water?" say to yourself: "people walk across that bridge every day, yet it's never fallen into the water."

Let go of your anxiety or anger

Exercise is a good way to release emotional tension. Take a walk or run. Physical activity releases serotonin, which helps you relax and feel better. You should, however, avoid physical activities that include the display of rage, such as pounding walls or screaming. This has been demonstrated to promote sentiments of rage since it reinforces the emotions because being furious makes you feel good.

Visualize yourself being relaxed

This tip asks you to put the breathing skills you've learned into practice. Close your eyes and visualize yourself calm after taking a few deep breaths. Visualize your body relaxed, and imagine yourself navigating a stressful or anxiety-inducing circumstance by remaining calm and attentive.

You can think back to that image when you're anxious if you create a mental image of what it looks like to be calm.

Give it some thought

Have a mantra ready to utilize in stressful situations. Just make sure it's one you'll find useful. "Will this matter to me this time next week?" says Dehorty. or "How critical is this?" or "Am I going to let this person/situation take my peace?"

This permits the mind to shift focus and helps you to "reality test" the event. When we are nervous or angry, we become hyper-focused on the source of our anxiety or anger, and sensible thoughts leave our heads. These mantras provide an opportunity for rational thought to return and lead to a better end.

Listen to some music

When you feel your anxiety rising, put on some headphones and listen to your favorite music. Music may have a highly relaxing effect on both your body and mind.

Change your focus

Leave the situation, turn around, walk out of the room, or go outside. According to my counseling experience, using this exercise gives you more time to make better decisions. When we are anxious or furious, we do not think clearly; instead, we participate in survival thinking. This is good if our lives are truly in danger, but if they aren't, we want our best thinking, not survival instincts.

Allow your body to unwind

When you're anxious or furious, every muscle in your body may feel rigid (and they probably are). Progressive muscle relaxation can help you relax and center yourself. Lie down on the floor with your arms out by your sides. Check that your feet are not crossed and that your hands are not made into fists. Begin with your toes and tell yourself to let them go. Slowly work your way up to your body, reminding yourself to let go of each part of your body until you reach your head.

Write it down

If you're too upset or anxious to talk about it, take out a journal and write down your feelings. Don't be concerned with complete sentences or punctuation; just write. Writing allows you to clear your mind of negative thoughts. You can take it a step further and create an action plan to maintain your calm once you've finished writing.

Get some fresh air

The temperature and air circulation in a space can make you feel more anxious or angry. If you're feeling tight and the environment is hot and stuffy, you may get a panic attack. Get away from the situation as soon as possible and go outside, even if only for a few minutes. Not only will the fresh air help you relax, but the change of environment may also assist in breaking up your nervous or furious thought process.

Fuel your body

Many of these approaches will not work if you are hungry or dehydrated. That's why it's critical to take a break and eat something, even if it's just a small snack.

Relax your shoulders

If your body is strained, your posture will most likely suffer. Sit up straight, take a deep breath, and let your shoulders fall. You can do this by focusing on bringing your shoulder blades together and then down. This causes your shoulders to drop. Take a few deep breaths. This is something you can do numerous times a day.

Use a centered object

When you're nervous or angry, you spend a lot of energy on nonsensical thoughts.

Find a "centering object," such as a little stuffed animal, a polished rock you keep in your pocket, or a locket you wear around your neck while you're calm. When you're feeling anxious or frustrated, tell yourself that you're going to touch this object. This helps to center you and calm your mind. For example, if your supervisor is making you nervous at work, gently stroke the locket around your neck.

Recognize pressure spots to alleviate rage and anxiety

Receiving a massage or getting acupuncture is an excellent approach to deal with anxiety and anger. But finding time in your day to make it happen isn't always easy. The good news is that you can use acupressure on yourself to get immediate anxiety relief.

This approach entails applying pressure to specific places on the body using your fingers or hand. The pressure soothes your body and relieves tension. One place to start is the crease formed by the inside of your wrist and your hand. For two minutes, press your thumb on this spot, and this can assist in easing stress.

Chapter Four
THE PEACEFUL PARENTING APPROACH

Laura Markham, Ph.D. clinical psychologist and author of the bestselling book "Peaceful Parent, Happy Kid: How to Stop Yelling and Start Connecting," published in 2012, founded the idea of peaceful parenting.

In a nutshell, her notion of peaceful parenting is divided into three central ideas:

1. managing emotions as a parent
2. connecting with your kids
3. coaching rather than punishing

This emphasis on attention permeates all aspects of peaceful parenting. This means that you are completely immersed in whatever is happening in your home and with your children.

Aside from that, you take the time to understand and honor your feelings, as well as any previous experiences or traumas that may have influenced how you behave to your children in difficult situations.

The goal is to improve behavior from the inside and to foster a solid parent-child attachment. Its goal is to provide children with the tools they need to recognize their own emotions and, as a result, make sound decisions as they grow up.

The three pillars of peaceful parenting

Peaceful parenting is the parenting style that I use and teach. Many parents choose the peaceful parenting technique because it feels good to be on the same team as your child and have less tension in the home. However, calm parenting is a long game. According to the research, setting limits rather than punishing our children helps them develop intrinsic motivation, resilience, empathy, and a strong internal sense of right and wrong.

Before we begin, please keep in mind that peaceful parenting is NOT an easy technique. It necessitates patience, self-awareness, and a significant amount of effort on our part as parents. It's arduous work. However, any seasoned peaceful parent will tell you that it is well worth it.

We said that peaceful parenting is based on three big ideas. Let's break them down one by one in detail.

Parental self-regulation

Parental self-regulation is a fancy way of expressing that we strive not to yell at our children or, worse, yell at ourselves when we are frustrated.

This is not to say that parents never become angry with their children. Of course, we will be upset from time to time. That's just part of what it's like to be human. When we are irritated, we strive to calm down so that we can respond to the circumstance and the child in front of us rather than reacting in anger.

Why it's significant?

Our children are terrified by yelling. Even if a youngster appears to be peaceful on the outside, research shows that they have increased heart rates and cortisol (stress) levels. We feel horrible about ourselves when we yell. This creates a vicious cycle: when we feel horrible about ourselves, we are more likely to be hijacked by our own strong emotions and yell the following time again. Furthermore, feeling horrible about yourself as a parent is not a pleasant experience!

Our relationship with our children suffers as a result of our yelling. Consider if you had a manager that was constantly shouting at you when you made a mistake. What would your reaction be to the person? I know I wouldn't be my best self in front of them, and I'd definitely avoid spending time with them. Furthermore, if we repeatedly damage our child's feelings and scare them, they will construct a small wall around their hearts.

Yelling causes our children to develop low self-esteem. If the person they love the most in the world is constantly yelling at them, they are more likely to believe they are a nasty person.

Poor self-regulation makes it difficult to employ any parenting strategy effectively. If we are irritated with our child, chances are there is something we need to do right then and there to help our child start doing ABC or stop doing XYZ. When our big sentiments take over, we are operating from our brain's fight-flight-or-freeze mode rather than our thinking brain mode. We can't effectively use any of the methods we could use to get our child to listen and comply if we can't use our thinking brain's executive function, planning, and logical cognitive capabilities.

We act in ways we subsequently regret as a result of poor self-regulation. When our thoughts and behaviors are hijacked by our strong emotions, the person in front of us appears to be the adversary, and we do or say things we regret.

Focus on connection and the relationship

Parenting becomes more enjoyable when there is a sense of connection. We didn't want to have children only to have someone to annoy and keep us on track with our daily routine! We decided to have children to bring more joy into our life. Of course, we adore our children, but when we feel connected to them, life becomes more joyful and sweet.

Parenting is made easier by connection. Our bond with our children is the most powerful tool we have for influencing them. We are hardwired for connection as humans. This keeps us safe from an evolutionary standpoint. Not only does connection motivate caregivers to watch out for children, but also we are more likely to follow people with whom we feel close since they are more likely to have our best interests at heart.

When children feel connected, it leads to more collaboration in the home. This is especially true for children with strong personalities. They may not want to do what you want, but they may do it for YOU.

You can easily notice it with teenagers. My then-15-year-old son informed me a few years ago that many of his pals ignored their parents' phone calls and texts and went home late, if at all.

"You're lucky I care about what you and Dad think," he continued.

He is correct. Having 'kids who care about what you think' is 90% of the parenting equation, especially as they become older.

Set limits with empathy instead of punishment

To get our children to do something or stop doing it, we have to employ empathetic limitations and support rather than punitive approaches.

We all have behavioral expectations for our children. For example, we expect them to arrive at the dinner table on time. We don't want children to pull the dog's tail or write on the walls with a marker.

When you call your child to dinner, he or she may continue to play; they simply can't stop themselves from pulling on the fluffy tail or sketching on the huge white canvas in the living room. When these things occur, there is a chasm between our expectations and reality. As parents, we feel powerless and annoyed by this gap. Traditional parenting use threats, penalties, or incentives to bridge the gap:

- "You're going to get a time out if you don't stop yanking on the dog's tail!"
- "You're going to pay the price if you don't..."
- "I'm putting away your pens for a week since you drew on the walls."
- "If you don't come right now, you won't be able to use the computer later!"

Let's try not to use threats, repercussions, or punishments to get our kids to close the gap between our expectations and reality in peaceful parenting. You can use the words "consequences" or "punishment," but they both mean the same thing. Punishment, often known as parent-imposed consequences, is defined as anything that intentionally makes a child feel terrible in order to modify their behavior.

I believe in peaceful parenting because I believe a child can learn without being made to feel guilty. Indeed, feeling miserable frequently gets in the way of learning! Punishment also harms our relationships with our children, fails to teach the lessons we intend to teach and is ineffective in the long run.

So, if threats and penalties aren't an option, how do we bridge the gap between our expectations of our child and reality? We employ gentle yet firm compassionate boundaries. The expectation itself serves as a limit: no drawing on the walls. It also includes the assistance we must provide our children in order for them to reach expectations. Support is frequently manifested as doing something to assist our child in meeting our expectations.

What do we need to do to help our child come to the table if it is expected that he or she will come to dinner when it is time? How can we help our children?

First, we must ensure that we are effectively capturing our child's attention. If your child hears you but refuses to stop playing, try one of our peaceful parenting strategies to support both your child and your limit. This is sometimes referred to as "How can I get them to... XYZ?"

Here are a few examples:

- Provide options. "Would you like to come right now or in 5 minutes?" "Do you want to walk, or do you want me to carry you?"
- To gain cooperation, try a win-win solution. Engage them in play by "flying" them to the table or inviting them to bring one of their Lego characters to "watch" them eat.
- Solicit assistance in resolving the issue. "You don't want to keep playing, AND it's time for dinner. How should we proceed?"

Your expectation or limit is not optional, which is why we refer to them as "firm" limits. However, rather than threatening or punishing your child, you will provide the assistance they require to get there.

What do we need to do to support the limit if it is 'no pulling the dog's tail' or 'no writing on walls'?

We may need to separate our child and the dog and ensure that they are always closely supervised so that we can swoop in if necessary. We may also need to relocate the markers so that our children cannot reach them unless we are present to supervise. We don't have to be nasty about it!

In fact, the more you can empathize with a child, the easier it is for him or her to accept the boundary. We must communicate to our children that we understand and are on their side, even if it means moving them away from the dog or putting the markers up high where they cannot reach.

How to follow the guidelines of peaceful parenting

It appears to be straightforward, doesn't it? Here's a breakdown of how each of these categories is divided.

Emotional regulation as a parent

First and foremost, tranquil parent examines their own emotions and subjectivities, shaping their attitude to various parenting scenarios.

You've probably considered it before. You notice your child tearing into the kitchen cupboard – yet again. And all you can think about is the horrifying disaster that will await you when they're through. You travel from zero to sixty in less than two seconds, and you may only see "red," which means "high alert."

Emotion regulation entails taking a deep breath and dissecting the circumstance at hand. Why is your child in the cupboard in the first place? Are they starving? Bored? Is that cabinet demanding to be broken into? Before yelling, consider your own emotions as well as the surrounding environment.

Dr. Markham frequently mentions fury as a secondary emotion to fear. So, when you take a step back, ask yourself, "What am I terrified of?" The answer isn't always obvious, and depending on the circumstances, it may be difficult to face.

Regulating your emotions creates an excellent model for your children to follow. Consider it the polar opposite of blowing your top. Even after taking inventory of your inner sentiments, even after you've been mindful, you can still feel and communicate anger. The difference is that you took a moment to collect yourself before reacting.

<u>Making contact with your children</u>

You may be thinking, "But I'm already really close to my child. Like literally. She's clinging to my leg 24 hours a day and won't let go."

This isn't about personal space, believe it or not. It's about the close relationship that parents and children have. When was the last time you truly felt connected to your child? Or what might be impeding you from feeling that way?

Dr. Markham offers some suggestions for how you might interact with your child:

- Attachment parenting, which entails emotional and physical connection, is being practiced with young babies.
- Every day, one-on-one "special" playtime. It doesn't have to be for an extended time; even 10 to 20 minutes can make a significant difference.
- When interacting with your children, turn off the television, tablets, phones, and other forms of technology.
- Make family time a priority each night, such as eating supper together.
- Hugs, snuggles, and other displays of affection are all ways to connect physically.
- Develop your unique routines for connecting with your child, such as snuggling for a few minutes before getting out of bed for the day.

Working on your relationship not only can make your youngster feel safer but also they learn to love themselves and will be able to love others consequently. Dr. Markham explains that connection is what "makes calm parenting possible" because children want to cooperate and behave when they are connected to their parents.

<u>Instead of commanding, try coaching</u>

This last concept, coaching vs. controlling, may be the most difficult to grasp. You may be wondering how your child will listen to you without repercussions or whether losing the ability to yell and punish would make you appear weak. However, it's worth noting that in peaceful parenting, cooperation and good behavior tend to follow after removing the power dynamic.

Coaching may provide your child with the tools they need to improve their behavior in ways that punishment or bribery cannot. When you take away your teen's iPhone, for example, they may become furious and resentful. If you bring to their notice what is causing a specific behavior before reprimanding them, the ultimate outcome can be helpful for all parties concerned.

As strange as it may sound, helping your child connect with their feelings is proved to be quite beneficial in the long run for better conduct. It's not just for you, either. Instead, the goal is to provide children with the vocabulary and ideas they need to navigate the world with greater emotional intelligence and make sound decisions. A peaceful family is simply a nice added benefit.

Practical tips to transition to peaceful parenting

Shifting your parenting style is a significant step, and you should expect some bumps while you and your family learn new ways of relating.

Even if your child occasionally "acts worse" than she would have previously, those bumps don't signal you're doing anything wrong. In truth, when your child acts out, she expresses feelings from the past, from when you yelled or chastised her, and she felt alone and misunderstood. It will require additional compassion from you, but your empathic response will heal those wounds and allow you all to move on.

Many parents may feel sorry for the way they behaved before discovering peaceful parenting. However, feeling horrible will not help you act "good" any more than it would assist your child. So let go of the guilt. After all, you're paying the price and making restitution now by assisting your child in healing those past hurt feelings.

Begin with yourself

You are the source of the "peace" in peaceful parenting. Specifically, your commitment to self-regulation of emotions. That is, when you are upset, you should stop, drop your agenda (temporarily), and breathe. You become more aware of what your body is feeling, which allows you to remain more mindful and avoid being hijacked by anger. You refuse to act on that frantic "fight or flight" emotion that portrays your child as the adversary. You postpone action whenever possible until you feel more at ease.

This requires work, both with your child and in general, as you become more conscious of your thoughts and feelings. It's not an easy task. In fact, it's quite tricky. Every time you do this, though, you are increasing gray matter in your brain, which aids in developing impulse control. And you're removing the triggers that cause you to lose it, so you don't get upset as frequently.

Concentrate on connecting

Peaceful parenting does not operate in the absence of connection. So, before you do anything else with your child, start by strengthening your bond. Otherwise, you'll stop punishing your child, but they will still be unmotivated to "do the right thing," and you'll just witness more testing behavior. Spend at least 15 minutes each day interacting one-on-one with each child, simply following his lead and pouring your love into him. You'll be astounded at how differently he responds to your requests.

Explain what is going on

Wait until you see more collaboration and connection. Then, start a conversation.

"When you broke the rules, I used to shout at you and send you to your room. Have you noticed that I'm yelling a lot less lately? I'm sorry I developed such a poor habit of yelling. I love you, and I know you work very hard. No matter what, you do not deserve to be yelled at. Nobody does.

We still follow the same set of rules. As a result, it is never acceptable to lie, break commitments, or bother your sisters. But don't you believe you'll learn more from cleaning up your messes and fixing your mistakes than from getting punished? So, if you destroy something, including a relationship with a member of our family, we expect you to fix it. We will always be available to support you. And when you're upset, we want to help you with whatever issue you're experiencing. Let's start with a family meeting to discuss what household rules are vital to us."

Request cooperation

"The essential rule in my house is that we treat each other with kindness. I will try very hard not to yell at you and instead listen and be kind to you. Do you believe you can follow this guideline while also being kind to your sister?" From the statements above, you can infer that you can count on your child about NOT losing control or breaking the kindness rule. Resist the urge to use this to justify your own ranting; after all, you are the role model.

Assist and serve as a role model for win-win solutions

"I know your younger sister can get on your nerves at times, and she always wants to play with your stuff. I understand that it irritates you greatly. You have earned the right to keep your things safe. However, it is not acceptable to yell at or hit your sister. Why don't we collaborate to find a safe spot for your treasures where your sister won't be able to access them? And if you become irritated with her, what other options do you have except yelling?"

Continue to set boundaries

You become more adaptable as you experience things through your child's eyes more frequently, which is a wonderful thing. But you'll still need to set a lot of boundaries. The trick is to set the boundary BEFORE you become upset while still empathizing with his point of view. "Don't you wish you didn't have to stop playing and get ready for bed? I'm sure you'll want to play all night every night when you grow up, don't you? And now it's time for you to take a bath."

Recognizing your child's point of view while you set the limit is what encourages them to work with you.

Instruct on reparations

If you've been punishing your child, you'll feel incomplete if he breaks a rule and you don't penalize him. Instead, train yourself to think in terms of repair.

Have a private conversation with your child about what happened after everyone has cooled down and feels reconnected. Be patient, listen carefully, and truly empathize. That is what will get him through it. "You got angry when he did that... I understand." Resist the impulse to instruct until your child has opened up and revealed all of the issues that have prompted him to behave out. Then, without shaming or blaming him, point out the cost of his behavior. "You severely damaged your brother's feelings when you said it to him.... I'm curious if it made him feel less close to you."

Ask your child if there is anything he can do to help repair the damage. "I wonder what you could do to help your brother mend things?"

Refrain from punishing yourself or forcing an apology. Instead, encourage your child to recognize that he can make up for his faults. "You do realize we always clean up our messes, don't you? This is simply a different kind of a mess, similar to spilled milk. I'm confident you'll come up with just the appropriate way to make things right with your brother.... I can't wait to find out."

As with cleaning up spilled milk, the process of cleaning up his messes will educate him that he doesn't want to cause those harms in the first place. Just keep in mind that this isn't a punishment. He needs to repair it, and he needs to do it before the end of the day, but what he chooses to do to help his sibling is entirely up to him. Of course, if your child's "fixing" is perceived by the sibling as insufficient for the offense, you will need to interfere once more. After all, the goal of mending is to make things right with the person you've wronged.

What if your youngster is unwilling to repair? That suggests he needs more assistance from you to heal his hurt before he can move on to repair. Check to make sure you're not lecturing and that you truly see his point of view, so he feels heard and can work through his strong feelings. If old resentments are causing a chip on his shoulder, make a promise to yourself that you will begin the repair process today to melt those resentments.

Be prepared for feelings

When children are disciplined, they learn that the strong emotions that cause them to misbehave land them in hot water, so they develop the practice of shoving those "bad" impulses down. Of course, that doesn't work. Jealousy, irritation, and need remain in your child's emotional backpack, ready to burst at the slightest provocation. The only reason your child is keeping them hidden is that they are terrified. So, once you stop punishing, those emotions will inevitably pop up to be healed. As a result, when you begin punishing, you should anticipate seeing much stronger emotions. You will witness less anger if you can make it safe for your youngster to show you their more vulnerable side.

However, there may be more acting out for a brief period. When your children "act out," they are expressing some feelings that they cannot articulate verbally. "All those times you yelled at me, and I was so afraid...," for example. "I pretended not to care, but I was afraid on the inside. That fear is still inside me, and it eats me away and makes me feel awful. So I lash out to keep those feelings at bay." Since no child in the world could express their feelings this way, they just act out.

You are not facing a personal difficulty by acting out. Emotions are never a problem; humans will always experience strong emotions. Of course, this does not give your child permission to harm others. Train yourself to see disobedience as a cry for help and to set limits gently and patiently to manage conduct. The idea is to help your child in working through the hurts and concerns at the root of their anger so that they no longer drive their behavior. Connection, laughter, and tears are the most acceptable ways to accomplish this.

Create a safe environment

Maintain your calm when your child expresses their displeasure and don't take it personally. The more caring and welcoming you are, the more comfortable they will feel to show you the woundedness that lies beneath the anger. (Note that anger is the body's battle response to frightening feelings.)

It is therapeutic to express one's feelings and concerns. Once they share them with you – and they don't even have to know what they're about or use words to do so – those painful sensations will fade, and they won't need that chip on their shoulder to protect themselves.

If your child is locked in anger, provide more safety for them by being as sensitive as possible about what is truly bothering them. If it doesn't make them cry, and they remain angry, it's a sign that they need more daily empathy, as well as more daily laughter with you. Both foster trust.

Use a story to help your children make sense of their experience

"I was having a terrible time when you were a kid. I screamed a lot. I couldn't think of anything else to do. That scared you. So you got really angry at times. Nowadays, I try my best not to yell and to be courteous. You don't get scared like that. And you're getting better at showing me when you're upset, terrified, or angry. In our family, we work together to solve problems. Everyone gets upset now and then. We make an effort to listen to and be kind to one another. Then we always fix problems between ourselves. There is always room for more love."

All children, as we did once, learn to understand and navigate their emotions through the use of words and stories. Just make sure you sympathize rather than analyze, so they feel understood rather than invaded or scolded.

Model apologies

Expecting repair before the end of the day enables your child to heal relationships, which works far better than pushing your child to apologize in the heat of the moment. This breeds resentment. However, if you model apology yourself, your child will learn from you. So, when something goes wrong, accept as much blame as possible to demonstrate how to step up and accept responsibility.

"I observe two upset children. I'm sorry I wasn't there to help you work this out before you both got angry and began punching ... and then I became concerned that someone would be hurt, so I began yelling as well. I'm very sorry. Let's all try again. I understand you don't want to attack each other since it hurts. And I can hear how angry you are. Let's start afresh so you can tell each other what you need without getting into a fight."

There is no guilt or shame here. You're just trying to make it easier for everyone involved to analyze and admit how they may have contributed to the problem.

<u>Be prepared for setbacks</u>

Because you're human, you're not perfect. Just as you do for your child, compassion for yourself is the key to making this change. Expect some days to be quite tricky. Expect to make errors. Parenting is complex, and this type of parenting is even more difficult to begin with. But it becomes easier when you acquire new methods that function better and rewire your brain. Even though it's difficult, you're healing your child's past wounds—as well as your own—so you'll notice a change. Simply put, there is less drama and more love.

<u>Make the commitment every morning</u>

This style of parenting is what I stick to regularly. Every morning, as a mother myself, I have to decide not to yell, be calm, and choose love. And there's something incredibly liberating about that. When I make mistakes or stumble, I apologize to my children; I notice that when they accept my apologies, they feel empowered and generous in spirit. This affects their interactions with one another; there are more friendly words and gestures, more "I'm sorry," and more "Don't worry, I know it wasn't your fault" than previously. There are days when things get difficult, but I genuinely believe that something is changing deep within our hearts, and that we are growing closer together when we choose love. When my child is having a tantrum, I hug him and sincerely tell him that I hear his pain and that I will help him work through it.

Chapter Five
SETTING BOUNDARIES

Many households now have "mini-democracies" in which children's views and opinions are equal to those of their parents. In some households, the child's voice takes over completely. In some houses, certain parents would even completely disregard their own wants to make their child happy.

The pendulum has always swung from focusing on children's behavior to focusing on children's emotions, which fortunately happens nowadays. However, there has been an exponential growth in anxiety disorders in children and teenagers as a result of this. Although it is critical for children's emotions to be acknowledged and validated, a parent must remain in command in order to provide a secure and stable environment for their children. Parents, in particular, are responsible for establishing boundaries in the home to promote an environment in which their children can be heard and encouraged to develop patience, self-awareness, and so on.

Reasons to Set Boundaries With Kids

Here are four reasons why parents must be "in command" of setting boundaries to set the tone for their children's emotional development:

1. Parental boundaries provide children with a sense of security.

Anxiety is reduced when secure boundaries are established by the parent (rather than negotiated by the youngster). Meal times, bed times, homework time, chores, and screen time that are set and controlled by the parent create regularity in a child's life. Predictability eliminates uncertainty, which lowers anxiety.

Parents should not prioritize a child's sense of security over their ability to express themselves. Setting boundaries does not make you a nasty or unfair parent, even if your child says so to you in anger at the time. When a youngster attempts to negotiate a later bedtime, it jeopardizes the child's sense of security by allowing the child to believe they have more authority than the adult.

2. Children's prefrontal lobes are underdeveloped.

In other words, because a child's brain is not completely matured, they should not be granted decision-making authority over adults. "Magical thinking" predominates among kids aged two to seven. Children are amazing and full of wonder because of their "magical thinking." However, it also implies that young toddlers are not prepared to make major decisions, such as whether to eat peanut butter & jelly or grilled cheese.

School-aged children between the ages of eight and eleven are mostly concrete in their thinking. This is why elementary school children adore rules and prefer a black-and-white world. Structure, after all, ensures predictability and security. Children do not begin to develop more abstract and complex thinking until they are 12 years old. This is why adolescence is a better period to experiment with norms and boundaries. Nonetheless, parents must remain "in charge" of setting boundaries with their adolescents because they are still building prefrontal controls for impulsivity, decision-making, and problem-solving, despite all the hormonal changes.

Even as we learn more about brain development, we appear to be losing sight of our children's specific developmental stage and what level of choice is good for them to have. Many parents today bargain with their five-year-olds as if they are mini-adults, believing that their children comprehend all the nuances of why regulations alter and move.

3. Narcissism and entitlement are disrupted by parental boundaries.

For many families, a child's emotions, demands, and desires can take over the entire day rather than the other way around. In small children, narcissism is acceptable and developmentally appropriate.

However, unless the early-development narcissism is interrupted, children will continue to believe that the world revolves around them and will grow into narcissistic adults. Parental boundaries assist children in maturing, understanding that they cannot always get their way; they should finally become more patient and mature. Children can learn to cope with disappointment by knowing that there is a limit to how much comfort and pleasure their parents will provide. As a bonus, the mild disappointment often caused by boundaries can also help children develop empathy. Understanding the definition of "limits" encourages children to feel more connected to the real world.

It's completely fine and fair for a parent's reasoning to end here: "I'm making this decision because I'm the parent, and you're the child." When done gently but firmly to encourage a child's sense of safety and security, the concept of a parent being "in charge" is not a power trip.

4. We all learn from a bit of struggle.

Kids must struggle in any developmental endeavor, from walking to talking, to learning to read or ride a bike. The struggle is how we grow and learn to master new skills. Children who are raised with the belief that they will always be "in command" want things to be simple. They also assist parents in removing difficulties and resolving disappointments (sometimes called helicopter parenting). A responsible parent understands that a child's struggle with a limit or regulation is acceptable, beneficial, and healthy. It's okay if they have to turn off their video game to read, eat more vegetables, or do extra duty to help mom.

Parents who set boundaries are not attempting to make their child happy at the moment (though they occasionally do!). Rather, and more crucially, they are attempting to help their child develop abilities that will allow them to successfully enter the world at the age of 18.

How to Set Healthy Boundaries with Children

We all know that children require limitations and boundaries! But it's a different story when it comes to establishing and enforcing such boundaries. Try telling a child "no" if you haven't already.

It is difficult for many parents to set limits, especially if you have never done so before! We love our children as parents, and we would never want to see them angry because of something we did or could have prevented!

Nonetheless, we must remind ourselves that setting limits for our children is essential. It will not only benefit them, but it will also make our parenting journey much easier as our children grow! We all need to learn what is expected of us, and childhood is the finest time to do it. Furthermore, it is ideally aligned with their growth goals. At this stage, all children are seeking to explore their environment, intently watching their surroundings, replicating behaviors they observe, noticing cause-and-effect links, and formulating beliefs about norms based on what they see.

Don't be concerned if they're too young to understand such boundaries. Learning about boundaries at a young age equips children with the skills needed to manage future relationships, making them less likely to do things that make others uncomfortable. It all comes down to recognizing what is and is not appropriate behavior. This crucial life skill is one that you, as parents, must teach your children, as well as one that they must learn and retain.

Then there's the crucial question: how can we healthily teach children boundaries so that they may learn while still understanding that we love them? Here are some pointers!

Establish clear and direct rules

There are few ambiguities or loopholes as a result of this. Your kid is less likely to cross the line because the rules are easy for them to follow and grasp. Remember that they, too, are still honing their language skills! Your wording should be direct and limited in scope and NOT open-ended or open for misinterpretation.

Let's have a look at two examples:

- "Why don't you complete your food before you play with your toys?" A says.
- "Please complete your dinner before playing with your toys," says B.

The second instruction is brief, to-the-point, and powerful, and it is more successful in conveying your message to your child. Not only will your child learn what you want immediately, but they will also be able to tell how steadfastly you adhere to these guidelines.

Consistency is essential!

Consistency breeds familiarity. There is structure and discipline at home by constantly enforcing standards, both of which are vital components of effective parenting. It would be easier for your children to understand how to keep inside the boundaries you set for them. Furthermore, they will understand that you are serious about setting boundaries, which will help them learn to be accountable for their behavior. Hopefully, this will make them reconsider before committing a (possible) offense!

Appropriate body language

We've all heard that verbal language only accounts for a small portion of how compelling a message is. This also applies to teaching children boundaries!

Make appropriate eye contact, talk in a firm voice, and maintain a neutral facial expression when instructing or scolding your child. Consider making eye contact at their level, which requires you to kneel down. This is done to keep kids from being overly intimidated.

Do not try to reprimand them while still laughing or smiling at them; if you are not convinced when someone does this to you, chances are your child will not be either. Your child will realize that you mean what you say if what you say is consistent with what you do. This increases their likelihood of adhering to the established bounds.

Remain determined and follow through on the consequences

Our children will never be upset in a perfect world, and not with us, at any rate.

However, know that it's okay if your child is upset with you when you're setting boundaries. They must understand what is and is not acceptable behavior. Furthermore, the experience can teach kids how to cope with negative emotions in a healthy, sensible manner. These teachings you have for children are quite important, so don't feel guilty about it.

It may be tempting to retract anything you've said or done, but remember that hollow threats are not the way to address problems. While empty threats may keep your child happy for the time being, they also show your youngster that you are not serious about setting boundaries, and they may choose to defy these limits in the future.

Recognize when they have adhered to the boundaries you have set!

This is an excellent approach to demonstrate to your child that you still love them even if they have done something bad! When they do anything nice, congratulate them and thank them for their efforts. Children enjoy being noticed and applauded for their efforts, especially when it comes from their parents! They will feel loved and appreciated, and as a result of this, they will be more inclined to adhere to these boundaries to relive these wonderful experiences! Positive reinforcement is quite effective at keeping a child's good behavior.

Establish developmentally appropriate goals

Recognize what can be done at different ages and what might be too advanced for your child. This protects you from having unrealistic expectations and will spare you a lot of heartaches later on.

Look up healthy expectations you can have for your child and use them as yardsticks for their development. You can keep track of their progress and inform them of their success! This can also serve as motivation for them to continue respecting your boundaries and engaging in prosocial behavior.

Don't give them too much power and authority in the family

Simply said, do not spoil your kids. When children are given too much power and control in the family, they acquire an exaggerated sense of influence and authority. The lines you've drawn for them become hazy. They may feel empowered to push the limitations you've established and will be less likely to follow through on what you've told them. This effectively lays the groundwork for future parent-child conflicts and power struggles as they grow older.

Worse, if not curtailed early on, it may become more difficult to set boundaries on your child when they enter puberty, a stage strongly associated with independence-seeking and identity-formation.

Setting Boundaries with a High Conflict Co-Parent

Ending a relationship with a conflict-prone spouse can be difficult on many levels. If you have children, one of the most arduous challenges will be figuring out how to work together as co-parents. You may have ideas about how you want to parent in the future, and these views may converge with those of the other parent.

Concerns about parenting children with a high-conflict co-parent are not uncommon or unfounded, but they can complicate matters for everyone involved, including your children. It can be difficult to even bring up the issue of developing a parenting approach without this person's willingness to collaborate. You may have reservations about working with your ex-spouse or partner, worrying that doing so may lead to disputes, wounded emotions, or further complications between you two. However, without some level of cooperation, your shared parenting is going downhill

Having a high conflict co-parent may make it more challenging to raise children together, but setting some boundaries between yourself and the other parent can help you stay secure and make it simpler to manage your shared parenting. Here are some suggestions on how you might work with a high-conflict co-parent to establish boundaries.

<u>Adhere to the parenting plan</u>

It will require much work to reach an agreement on a parenting plan in a high conflict co-parenting environment. That's often the case because conflicts and miscommunications can create significant barriers for parents attempting to figure out how to raise their children in the future. While mediation might help in some circumstances, parents may find themselves settling their arrangement in court in many cases where there is a conflict.

Whatever method you use, after you've decided on a strategy, commit to adhering to it. Hit the crucial points in your strategy, such as timing, expenses, how you'll make decisions together, and so on. Follow the parameters outlined in your parenting plan so that you have something concrete to back up your behavior. This will assist in decreasing the possibility of causing conflict by doing something that your co-parent believes is incorrect.

You're less likely to have a fight if you have defined limits. Furthermore, if your co-parent is the one who is unable to follow the parenting plan and adhere to its boundaries, you try to stick to it. If your co-disrespect parent's for the plan is causing problems for you and your kid, bring it to the attention of your attorney or any reputable family law specialists you work with. They will be able to advise you on how to proceed in this case.

Think about parallel parenting

Parallel parenting may be an effective technique to consider when your co-parent cannot collaborate, and communication is challenging. Parallel parenting is similar to co-parenting but with additional boundaries. One of these limits will be to isolate yourself from your co-parent on some level by not speaking directly with each other. You will limit your interactions to only what is essential for your children. You may not realize that parallel parenting does not have to persist indefinitely, but it will have a huge impact on how you handle your shared parenting from the start.

When parallel parenting, you may discover that you follow a very specific parenting strategy. This will urge each parent to adhere to the parenting plan while reducing the possibility of conflict caused by direct communication. As a result, you should organize parenting time exchanges in a monitored place, and you should avoid attending exchanges together.

You may still need to communicate on occasions, such as during child-related emergencies or when making important decisions, but you will not do so in the same ways you did previously. Written communication is frequently more comfortable in high tension co-parenting circumstances because it allows parents to maintain a physical buffer between themselves. While this is true, vagueness or harsh phrases in emails and text messages can often lead to conflict.

Keep your private life private

When an intimate relationship ends, emotions run high. Even if you wanted it to be done, you're probably still in pain after the breakup. However, in order to avoid being harmed or going back into a poor or toxic relationship, you must establish some emotional boundaries.

Keep your personal life to yourself if you want to keep your emotions in check when it comes to your co-parent. The only things you should discuss are those related to your children and nothing else. If your co-parent begins to inquire about your personal life, politely decline to discuss it. Consider not seeing this group of individuals for a while if you have mutual friends with your co-parent. You may even inform your friends as to why you are withdrawing from their social circle.

If social media has been a source of contention in the past, try blocking your co-accounts parent's or temporarily deactivating your pages. By not allowing your co-parent to stalk you on social media, you are setting limits on what your co-parent knows about your personal life. Maintaining these boundaries will help you better control the facts about your personal life that the co-parent knows, which will safeguard you in various ways.

<u>Keep an eye out for traps</u>

You should do everything you can to make boundaries between your co-parent and your personal life, and you should do the same for the other parent and their life. One of the numerous dangers you may encounter in this position is becoming overly interested in your co-parent's life.

Your high conflict co-parent may try to entice you into conflict by pressing your emotional buttons, or they may even harass you directly or indirectly. This could involve sending you hurtful remarks online or spreading rumors about you. As a result, commit to establishing a boundary that will keep you from falling into these conflict traps.

Limit your time on social media and avoid viewing anything that may be about your co-parent. If your co-parent sends you a harsh message, don't respond unless you have to. Limit your conversation to topics related to your children.

Tell your friends not to listen if you hear from them that your co-parent is spreading rumors about you. Explain the problem to your co-parent and how you feel hearing that they are spreading rumors. If you believe your co-parent has gone too far or has been doing this for an extended period, speak with a professional right away. This may be your attorney or, in the worst-case scenario, the police.

Talk with someone

It is difficult to get through a divorce or separation with a high-conflict partner on your own. Impose boundaries to protect yourself from the other parent, but don't set limits that prohibit you from getting the care you need.

Talk to close friends and family members you trust enough to express your feelings. Also, don't be afraid to seek the advice of a professional, such as a counselor or therapist. In times like this, these people are trained to help you deal with your emotions and maintain your emotional health. Counseling or therapy sessions can certainly help you in breaking down emotional barriers that may be preventing you from attaining your full potential in this new stage of your life.

Maintain contact with your attorney, especially if you are still dealing with disagreement with your co-parent. They can advise you on how to protect yourself and your children from harm caused by high-conflict situations.

Setting boundaries with a high conflict co-parent may sound easier than done, but remember that it is well worth the effort. Make a parenting plan and commit to following through on it. Set communication boundaries and decide how to deal with the occasions when you do need to chat. Maintain your privacy when it comes to your personal life, and don't fall into traps that make you curious about your co-parent's personal life.

Finally, do not set limits for yourself when it comes to requesting help when you believe you require it.

Chapter Six
DEALING WITH TANTRUMS

The first step in dealing with tantrums is to understand them. That is not always as simple as it sounds because tantrums and meltdowns can be caused by a variety of factors, including fear, frustration, wrath, and sensory overload, to mention a few. And, because a tantrum isn't a particularly obvious method to communicate (despite being a powerful means to gain attention), parents are frequently left in the dark about what's causing the behavior.

A tantrum might be seen as a child's reaction to a circumstance that they can't handle in a more mature way, such as by talking about how they feel, making a convincing case for what they want, or just doing what they've been asked to do. Instead, they are overcome with emotion. If acting out their emotions in a dramatic way — sobbing, yelling, stomping the floor, striking the wall, or slapping a parent — gets them what they want (or gets them out of whatever they were trying to avoid), it's a habit your child may grow to rely on.

This is not to say that tantrums are deliberately willful or even voluntary. However, it does imply that they are a learned response. So, with a tantrum-prone youngster, the goal is to help them unlearn this behavior and instead learn other, more mature methods to handle a troublesome situation, such as compromise or complying with parental expectations in exchange for some good reward.

Make an evaluation

The first step is to create a mental image of what causes your child's tantrums. This is referred to as a "functional assessment" by mental health professionals, and it entails looking at what real-life conditions appear to trigger tantrums — especially what happens immediately before, during and after the outbursts that may contribute to them occurring again.

A detailed examination of a child's tantrum pattern may show an issue that requires attention: a traumatic incident, abuse or neglect, social anxiety, ADHD, or a learning disorder. When children have meltdowns beyond the age range for which they are normal, it is typically a sign of discomfort they cannot handle. That effort crumbles at periods when kids need self-discipline they don't yet have, such as moving from something they enjoy to something challenging for them.

Most kids who have regular meltdowns do so in fairly predictable, limited situations: when it's time for homework, sleep, or when it's time to stop playing. The trigger is usually being asked to perform something unpleasant to them or quit doing something enjoyable. Something that is not entertaining and needs them to regulate their physical activity, such as a long car ride, a religious service, or seeing an old relative, is a common trigger for meltdowns in children with ADHD.

Observed behavior

Because parents frequently find tantrums intolerable, especially in public, the child may implicitly learn that throwing a tantrum can help them get their way.

It develops into a conditioned response. Even if it only works five out of ten times, the intermittent reinforcement makes it an extremely strong acquired behavior. As a result, children will continue to act in this manner in order to obtain what they desire.

One of the functional assessment purposes is to determine whether some tantrum triggers can be eliminated or modified so that they are less problematic for the child. We can't make it go away if putting on the shoes or leaving for school is the trigger. However, we may occasionally adjust the way parents and other caregivers manage a situation to defuse it. This could mean giving children more significant notice that a job is expected of them or organizing troublesome tasks in ways that lessen the chance of a tantrum.

Anticipating those triggers and altering them so that the kid can engage in that activity is critical. For example, suppose a child's homework is really tough for them due to underlying attention, organization, or learning challenges. In that case, they may have outbursts shortly before they're supposed to begin their homework. So the question to ask parents is: How can we make homework more enjoyable for the children? I would say we can offer them regular pauses, help them in areas where they are struggling, organize their work, and break bigger tasks into smaller parts.

Another goal is to evaluate whether the child's behavior expectations are developmentally appropriate for his age and maturity level. We must ask ourselves: can we change the environment to better match the child's skills and support development toward maturation?

Parents must realize two things: first, preventing a tantrum before it starts does not imply "caving in" to a child's demands. It entails distinguishing the unpleasant tantrum response from other concerns, such as complying with parental requirements. Second, by lowering the chance of a tantrum response, you eliminate the possibility of reinforcing that behavior. When children do not throw a tantrum, they learn to deal with their wants, desires, and problems more maturely, and this learning encourages acceptable reactions. Fewer tantrums now equate to fewer tantrums later.

Reacting to tantrums

When tantrums occur, the parent's or caregiver's reaction influences the likelihood that the behavior will occur again. There are numerous guidelines available to help parents in responding consistently and in ways that will reduce tantrum behavior in the future. They range from the fundamental "Collaborative & Proactive Solutions Approach," pioneered by Ross Greene, to step-by-step parent-training programs such as "Parent-Child Interaction

Therapy and Parent Management Training." They always begin with parents resisting the impulse to terminate the tantrum by giving the child what they want when they tantrum. For non-dangerous outbursts, the goal is to ignore the behavior and withdraw all parental attention because even negative attention or reaction, such as reprimanding or trying to persuade the kid to stop, has been shown to reward the behavior anyhow!

When a child attempts to calm down or, instead of tantrums, complies or provides a compromise, attention is diverted from the behavior you want to discourage and lavished on the conduct you want to encourage. By positively encouraging compliance and proper reactions to dissatisfaction, you're not only teaching your child some skills but also simultaneously, you're minimizing aggressive noncompliant tantrum behavior (because you can't comply with demand and tantrums at the same time).

One thing you don't want to do is try to reason with an upset child. When the child is not available, do not speak to them. You want to encourage a kid to practice negotiation skills when they aren't blowing up, and you aren't either. To have such impairments with immature children, you may need to teach them problem-solving skills and break them down step by step.

Exemplifying calm behavior

You must also demonstrate the type of negotiating you want your child to learn. Parents, too, need to take breaks. When you get angry, you should simply quit the situation. You can't solve problems while you're furious—your IQ reduces by roughly 30% when you're angry.

Being calm and clear about behavioral standards is vital because it allows you to interact with a youngster more successfully. So it's not as simple as, 'You must behave today.' 'You must sit during mealtime, keep your hands to yourselves, and speak only nice words,' you should say. These are extremely visible concrete behaviors that the child understands and that the parent can support with praise and rewards.

You and your child both need to develop what I call a self-soothing toolkit, which includes things you can do to cool down, such as slow breathing to relax, because you can't be peaceful and angry at the same time. There are other approaches, but the benefit of breathing is that it is always available to you.

Temper tantrums FAQ

You're in the grocery store with your child, and they have spotted a treat that you are not planning on purchasing. Suddenly, you find yourself in the midst of a gale-force rage tantrum.

What is the most appropriate response? Why do these emotional breakdowns occur? Can you stop them? Consider the following tantrum advice.

- Why do tantrums occur?

A tantrum is a young child's display of displeasure with their limitations or rage at not being able to get their way. Perhaps your youngster is having difficulty understanding something or completing a task. Perhaps your child lacks the words to describe their emotions. Frustration may cause an outburst, culminating in a temper tantrum.

When your child is sleepy, hungry, unwell, or has to make a transition, their irritation threshold is likely to be lower — and a tantrum more likely.

- Do young children purposefully throw tantrums?

Young children do not intend to annoy or disgrace their parents. Tantrums become a common way for them to show their dissatisfaction and can turn into a taught behavior later in life. Tantrums are likely to continue if you reward them with something your child wants or allow your child to get out of things by throwing a tantrum.

- Can tantrums be avoided?

There is no foolproof method for preventing tantrums, but there are many things you can do to encourage good behavior, even in the younger kids. For example:

<u>Maintain consistency</u>. Create a daily schedule for your child so that they know what to expect. Maintain as much of a routine as possible, including nap and sleep. If a child does not get enough rest or quiet time, their temper can flare.

<u>Make a plan.</u> Run errands when your child is neither hungry nor tired. Bring a small toy or food to keep your child entertained if you intend to wait in line.

<u>Allow your child to make responsible decisions.</u> Try not to say no to everything. Allow your toddler to make decisions to offer them a sense of control. "Would you like to wear your red or blue shirt?" "Would you rather have strawberries or bananas?" "Would you like to read a book or construct a skyscraper with your Lego bricks?"

<u>Reward positive conduct.</u> When your child acts in a satisfactory manner, give them extra attention. For example, when you see them share or follow orders, hug them or tell them how proud you are of them.

<u>Avoid situations that are prone to cause tantrums.</u> Never give your child things that are way too sophisticated for them. If your child begs for toys or sweets while you're shopping, avoid stores that sell

them. If your child becomes agitated in a restaurant, consider a location that provides speedy service.

- What is the best approach to handle a tantrum?

Staying calm is usually the best approach to deal with a tantrum. Your youngster may copy your behavior if you reply with loud, angry outbursts. Shouting at a child to calm down is also likely to aggravate the situation.

Instead, try to divert your child's attention. A different book, a different setting, or making a funny face could all help. If you've forced your child to perform anything against their will, offer to help. If you've told your child not to play in a certain place, consider showing them where it's acceptable to play.

If your child is punching or kicking someone or trying to run into the street, hold them until they calm down. When they have calmed down, explain or remind your rules collectedly.

- What if my child develops destructive or harmful tendencies?

If a tantrum goes out of hand, remove your child from the scene and impose a time-out, and consider the following:

Choose a location for a time-out. Place your kid in an uninteresting location, such as a chair in the living room or on the floor in the hallway. Allow your child some time to settle down. Consider giving them one minute of time-out for every year of their age.

Maintain your focus. Return your child to the prescribed time-out location if they begin to wander about before the time-out is over. While your child is in time-out, please do not respond to whatever they say.

Know when to call a time-out. When your child has calmed down, briefly explain why the time-out was necessary and why the behavior was improper. Then resume your regular activities.

However, don't overuse time-outs, or they won't work.

- When should you seek expert assistance?

Tantrums should become less common as your child's self-control increases. By the age of three and a half, most kids exhibit fewer tantrums. If your kid is causing harm to themselves or others, holds their breath to the point of fainting during tantrums, or has escalating tantrums after the age of four, discuss your concerns with your child's doctor. The doctor may look at physical or psychological factors that may be causing the tantrums.

Chapter Seven
UNDERSTANDING AND VALIDATING EMOTIONS

The way we understand and respond to our emotions significantly impacts our behavior, decisions, and how well we manage and enjoy life.

Emotional development in childhood

Consider all of the numerous emotions you experience daily, from surprise to embarrassment, elation to empathy, and how you react to each one. The way you deal with your feelings now is hugely different from how you dealt with them when you were thirteen, which is different from how you dealt with them when you were four.

Emotional development is a multifaceted process that begins in childhood and continues into maturity.

Emotional development begins with young children:

- learning what feelings and emotions are
- understanding how and why they occur
- acknowledging their feelings and those of others
- establishing appropriate coping mechanisms

Children's emotional life gets more complex as they grow and are exposed to new situations. It is critical for their emotional well-being that they develop abilities to handle a wide range of emotions.

Stages of emotional development

Babies begin to experience basic emotions such as joy, anger, sadness, and fear. Later in life, as children acquire a sense of self, they will experience more complex emotions such as shyness, surprise, elation, embarrassment, shame, remorse, pride, and empathy.

Physical reactions – such as their heart beating or butterflies in their stomach – and behavior are the major components of very young children's emotions.

Children can recognize feelings as they grow. Their thoughts are progressively influencing their emotions, and they become more conscious of their own emotions and are better able to recognize and comprehend those of others.

Emotional experience includes:

- physical reactions, such as heart rate, respiration, and hormone levels
- feelings that children recognize and learn to identify
- thoughts and judgments connected with feelings
- action cues, such as the desire to approach, flee or fight

Many factors influence how children communicate their emotions, both verbally and behaviorally.

Among these influences are:

- learning attitudes and views about suitable and inappropriate ways of expressing emotions from their parents and other family members
- how well children's emotional needs are typically met
- temperaments of children

- emotional behaviors acquired by youngsters through observation or experience
- the degree to which families and children are stressed in many ways

Why do youngsters require adult assistance?

At times, we can all feel overwhelmed. We learn over time what circumstances or experiences are likely to disturb us and how to manage our emotions when they do. We continue to learn about what bothers us and find new ways to deal with our emotions throughout our lives.

Children, like adults, might feel overwhelmed or out of control at times, but because they are younger, they have had less time and opportunity to learn how to manage their emotions. When adults listen to children's cues and help them in coping with their feelings of uncertainty, helplessness, or overwhelm, children feel comfortable and trust that they will be supported when they need it.

Children gradually learn to control their emotions for themselves due to their interactions with warm, attentive, and trusted adults. When children feel peaceful and protected, they are more likely to focus and sustain their attention, which is critical to their overall development.

Helping kids identify and express feelings

As we have seen, children, like adults, have complex feelings. They experience frustration, excitement, nervousness, sadness, jealousy, fear, worry, anger, and embarrassment.

However, most young children lack the vocabulary to express their emotions. Instead, they express their emotions in different ways available to them.

Children can convey their emotions through facial expressions, body language, behavior, and play. They may express their emotions in physical, inappropriate, or problematic ways at times.

Children begin developing the emotional abilities required to identify, express, and manage their feelings the moment they are born. They learn how to do so through social interactions and relationships with significant individuals in their lives, such as parents, grandparents, and caregivers.

When children learn to manage their emotions, they develop favorable attitudes and behaviors later in life.

Children who learn positive strategies to express and cope with their emotions are more likely to:

- Have good mental health and wellbeing
- Feel more competent, capable and confident
- Be empathic and supportive of others

- Perform better in school and their career
- Have more positive and stable relationships
- Display less behavioral problems
- Develop resilience and coping skills
- Have a positive sense of self

As a parent, you have a critical role in helping your children understand their emotions and behaviors. Children must be taught how to handle their emotions positively and constructively.

How to assist your child in developing emotional skills

Here are some ways you can help your child in learning about and expressing their emotions:

Pay attention to clues - It might be challenging to discern feelings at times. Look at your child's body language, listen to what they're saying, and observe their behavior to get a sense of how they're feeling. Understanding what they are feeling and why they are feeling that way allows you to help them better with identifying, expressing, and managing their feelings.

A feeling accompanies every behavior - Try to comprehend the meaning and emotion underlying your child's behavior. Once you understand what is causing the behavior, you may assist your child in finding different methods to express themselves.

Name the emotion - Give your youngster a label to help them name their emotions. Naming feelings is the first step in teaching children to recognize them. It enables your child to build an emotional lexicon, allowing them to express their emotions.

Recognize feelings in others – Make it a point to give people plenty of chances to identify their own emotions. You could ask your child to consider how someone else is experiencing. Cartoons or picture books are an excellent approach to talking about feelings and teaching children to recognize other people's emotions through facial expressions.

Be a role model - By watching others, children learn about feelings and how to express them appropriately. Demonstrate to your child how you feel in various situations and how you deal with those feelings.

Encourage with praise - Praise your child when they express their feelings in an appropriate manner. It not only normalizes having feelings and expressing them but also promotes the behavior, making it more likely that they will repeat it.

Listen to your child's feelings - Remain present and resist the urge of making your child's negative emotions disappear. Help your child with identifying and expressing their emotions so that they are heard.

When negative emotions are minimized or rejected, they frequently manifest in undesirable ways.

Using emotional validation as a parenting tool

Validation is a method of assuring someone that we comprehend them, and being understood is a necessary component of feeling connected and supported. When someone we care about understands us, it allows us to tune into ourselves and embrace our emotions as real and meaningful. This, in turn, promotes the development of self-compassion and the ability to empathize with others.

So, what should a parent do? Validate!

We can tell the difference when someone says to us: "Well, you could have done this instead" because we have shared an event that resulted in disappointment, vs. this reaction: "Wow, it is so sad that it didn't come out as you intended it to." While the first comment may have been made with the best intentions, it does not have the same impact as the second. We can realize how strong and influential validation can be simply by noticing the difference in how these two reactions make us feel about ourselves, the relationship, or others.

So, what exactly is validation? Simply said, validation is the act of assuring someone else that their experience is genuine. Given their experience, skills, and current circumstances, their point of view is understandable. Their experience is genuine and special for them, just as ours is so for us. While this may appear to be simple or easy to perform, it can be really tough to do as a parent at times. As parents, we believe that our role as protectors and teachers is critical to assisting our children in developing into successful, happy, and healthy adults.

As a result, a confrontation between these two forces is possible. Slowing down and walking in the shoes of our children who are naive, impulsive, and maturing in their ability to comprehend and manage their emotions while also trying to be a "good parent" who directs, teaches, and prepares a child for the world may be difficult to navigate. Sometimes we feel compelled to rush in and rescue or solve a situation for our children.

To figure this out, let's define what validation IS and IS NOT

<u>What validation IS</u>

- Listening quietly. Really listening! Put a stop to the chatter in your thoughts.
- Respect what your child says or expresses about their experience.
- Communicate that you understand your child's situation. Rephrase what your child has already

said.

- If you get it correctly, they'll nod, calm down, or elaborate further, feeling more at ease to share their story.
- If you get it wrong, you will be given further information to persuade you to get it right!
- Being interested in all of the aspects that contribute to the experience.

What validation IS NOT

- Judging
- Correcting
- Agreeing
- Teaching
- Arguing about why their experience is incorrect

As a parent, it can be especially tough to validate. When we believe that our child is being disrespectful or acting in a way that we do not respect, we may feel that affirming them is the last thing we want to do. At times, feeling unappreciated by our child leaves us longing to be recognized or understood.

What can I do to validate my child?

Validating your child's emotions can be challenging at times. Often, a child's distress causes parent distress, and it can be difficult to respond calmly at the moment. It can also be challenging to ignore your child's behavioral response. This is especially true when a child exhibits aggressive or destructive behavior, and in this case, ensuring safety takes precedence. Once safety has been restored, validation can take place.

When your child has a strong emotional reaction to a situation or stimuli, you should validate them. Being present with your child shows them that you care about them and that their emotions are not too big for you to handle. Sitting calmly nearby shows your child that you are present and ready to help when they are calm and ready to move on. It also demonstrates how to remain calm in stressful situations.

Another way to validate is to reflect back on their thoughts or feelings. "I realized you were frustrated when your brother wouldn't play with you," for example. "I know you worked very hard to put it together." When children struggle to express their thoughts or feelings, it is acceptable for parents to make educated guesses about their feelings. "I'm guessing you're feeling disappointed right now," you might say. It is also acceptable to be incorrect, and it still demonstrates that you are present and trying to comprehend.

Normalizing your child's feelings is another way to validate them. It can be comforting for children to know they are not alone and that others feel the same way they do, for example, "of course you're nervous about going to a new school – everyone is when they start something new." Saying "It's okay to be nervous" is another good option which demonstrates that you're validating your child's emotions as well as supporting them psychologically.

Even if you disagree with the reaction, validate it. Ignore the behavior and concentrate solely on the emotion. Once your child has calmed down, appreciate them for their ability to cope or persevere. "I know that was difficult for you," for example. "You were becoming increasingly irritated. I'm proud of you for persevering." Try to anticipate situations that may elicit strong emotions in your child and consider how you can validate them if they do.

Finally, remember to validate yourself and model positive coping skills. Children learn a lot about dealing with emotions by observing how adults respond to their own emotions. "I'm very disappointed," 6-year-old Kelly says. "It makes sense that I feel this way; however, this is difficult. I'm going to take a break and return to this when I'm more relaxed." This demonstrates emotional acceptance as well as healthy coping and can aid in the development of emotion regulation skills in children.

How do we unintentionally invalidate our children?

If we want to help our children effectively, we must first understand how parents unintentionally invalidate their children. We always keep in mind that any time a child's emotional experience is ignored, judged, or rejected, it is referred to as invalidation. Every parent has unintentionally invalidated their child's feelings. Many things that upset children appear trivial to adults, or the emotions can appear out of proportion to the situation. It can be difficult for an adult to put themselves in the shoes of a child at times.

When parents try to calm their children, they unintentionally invalidate them. It's difficult to see your child suffer and struggle. Parents will occasionally intervene to reassure their children that everything will be fine. Parents are also too quick to solve problems or suggest coping strategies. It can be difficult for parents to tolerate seeing their child in distress, so they push the problematic feelings away. Validation is not about solving problems or changing our children's emotional experiences; and it is about allowing your child to sit with and acknowledge their emotions.

Children are sometimes punished for their emotions or told that they are overreacting. When parents get nervous and tell their child to "just calm down," they only agitate them further. Dismissing a child's emotions as "acting like a baby" or "no reason to be angry" can make a child feel judged or rejected for their emotional experience, which they often have little control over.

When a child is repeatedly told that their internal emotional experience is incorrect, they feel less trusting and more out of control about their own internal experience, which can have long-term negative consequences. It can also harm a child's relationship with their parents.

Chapter Eight
PEACEFULLY RESOLVING CONFLICTS

Is it even possible to resolve conflicts peacefully?

Most of us grew up in families where disagreements were not handled appropriately. And when that happens, we not only don't learn conflict resolution skills, but we might also develop some quite bad behaviors in our adult lives. There's a reason Ram Dass' famous phrase is so well-known: "If you believe you're enlightened, go spend a week with your family"! We shudder at the thought of our children growing up and finding it difficult to be themselves around us.

Instead, we want to break generations of unhealthy relationship patterns, and we want to model excellent communication and conflict resolution skills for our children. We want our children to be able to be themselves and express their thoughts and feelings with confidence. We want them to know that we care about their thoughts and opinions, even if we disagree. And we want them to continue to share the difficult stuff with us throughout their adolescence and adulthood, knowing that we will always slow down, be present, and engage on a heart-to-heart level.

Healing our hearts

Wishing to handle disputes more skillfully is an admirable and ambitious goal, deserving of our dedication to a lifelong journey of change and growth. Love alone will not suffice to ensure that every family member feels properly seen, heard, and cared for. To make the dream of greater harmony a reality, we must figure out how to lessen the frequency of ruptures, minimize the hurt when disputes occur, and repair ruptures after conflicts.

The good news is that these are skills that can be acquired. Few parents grew up in families where their parents modeled appropriate emotional dialogues, so if this is unfamiliar and intimidating to you as a parent, remember that you are not alone! Mending our hearts and maintaining heart-to-heart talks is a path of healing previous wounds and learning to keep a soft heart and open mind despite the deeply programmed tendencies to shut down and re-affirm the old beliefs.

Parents quickly realize that wanting to do better than their parents isn't enough; there's a lot to learn and, in some cases, unlearn! Childhood behaviors and wounds can persist and be difficult to overcome! Differences in wants and needs are unavoidable, and misunderstandings are unavoidable. So, how can warm ties be preserved, how can all views be heard, and how can problems be addressed rather than simply hushed or buried?

Fight, flight, freeze, or please

It's natural to assume that the other person, whether a partner or a child, is blamed for the disagreement. When our versions of events disagree so radically from one another, it can be incredibly perplexing. And when attempting to discuss it results in defensiveness and upset, confusion results in distress and overwhelm! When we are stressed, our stress response is activated, and our deeply established reflexes to fight, flee, freeze, or please can kick in. And, while these reactions may have been all we could muster as youngsters, none of them have resulted in a satisfying outcome in our family now! It's not simply the great agony of feeling so misunderstood; it's also upsetting to see our loved ones not feeling heard or understood.

Let's analyze the tangled dynamics for a better understanding. If we're going to break the cycle of bad habits, we need to be very explicit about what a healthier approach to conflict looks like. To that end, understanding the various ways to conflict might help you find your way back to a more productive approach when you get off track.

Three prevailing approaches to conflict

The avoidant method is related to the flight or freeze stress response, the second to the fight stress response, and the third healthier option is to deliberately control one's stress response and bring connection into the conversation. The flight or freeze reaction seeks to avoid conflict; the fight stress response seeks to address conflict; and the third choice seeks to diffuse and resolve conflict via connection and calm, clear communication.

Drawbacks of seeking to prevent family conflicts

Avoidance, the technique for people whose stress response is flight or freeze, has several unintended implications. Attempting to avoid and prevent confrontations leaves family members feeling shut down, resentful, misunderstood, and often embarrassed. And it is precisely these feelings that contribute to increasing family conflict!

Rather than merely avoiding and discouraging conflict, which focuses on what should not happen, a much better strategy is to actively resolve problems as they emerge. This is more of a "fine, let's speak about it" response than a "why must you continually whine!" response. People who are continually trying to avoid conflict tend to focus on wishing others would not disagree or become offended. Which is both unrealistic and prone to exacerbate tensions when someone disagrees or becomes offended. Those who have had their voices hushed as children may find it difficult to speak up for themselves or others when faced with injustice, and also, they will probably be unable to cope with their child's upsets. Can you see the patterns?

The fight response

The fight response causes the child to be directly confrontational or aggressive, and it is very similar to the flight or freeze response in that the major message the youngster receives is that their arguments or upsets will not be accepted. It can entail yelling or raising one's voice to overpower the child. Overpowering can also occur when a parent is extremely analytical, culminating in a power struggle type dispute.

It's natural for parents to feel defensive, misunderstood, and unappreciated. Still, it's our responsibility as parents to demonstrate to our children that our concern for their feelings outweighs our need to be right. These more aggressive, assertive, or defensive responses make the other person feel that their acts and feelings are not tolerated. It can manifest as implementing punishments such as sending a child to their room (separation-based punishment), labeling, shaming, storming around, banging items, or slamming doors. This can be quite stressful for youngsters. And, tragically, it also affects parents' self-esteem, confidence, and dignity.

Managing emotions to avoid deflecting

When conflict arises, many adults, whether reacting from the fight or flight/freeze stress responses, tragically resort to destructive childhood behaviors such as denial, deflecting, becoming defensive, gaslighting, guilt-tripping, stonewalling, and even lying. These deflections are the polar opposite of being honest and straightforward about one's genuine feelings, and they often lead to the other person feeling blamed. If a person was not taught how to successfully and properly negotiate disagreements as a kid, these deflective methods might be all they have. Young adults who leave home without having learned good communication skills in the family, for example, may become unduly reliant on convenience and fast food.

People who learn how to manage their emotions during disagreements and how to speak effectively and fairly, will naturally teach their children good conflict resolution abilities. These abilities provide significant advantages in life.

How to maintain peace in the family

How can we best sustain family harmony and peace? Even within a family, there can be many competing demands, needs, preferences, and opinions in a single day. The parent wants their child to get dressed and ready to leave the house, but the child prefers to play with the toys and stay in their pajamas. When parents are extremely concerned with avoiding conflict at all costs, this can lead to denying and failing to address basic emotions and issues. Children pick up on an adult's dislike of conflict and may begin to control and repress their wants to express thoughts, feelings, and needs that they believe will cause difficulty to parent. Alternatively, they can go in the opposite direction and increase their dissatisfaction, knowing that their parent always bends and gives in to even the most outrageous demands.

Connection before correction

Working with difficulties skillfully encourages our children to do the same. A much healthier and more balanced approach emphasizes the importance of each individual feeling heard and understood. The best method to alleviate the anguish of detachment always includes bringing in some connection. Power disputes are often resolved through connection. The connection can be conveyed through empathy or affection, or it can be validated by showing the other person that their feelings are genuine even if we disagree. We may find some common ground by saying, "This is difficult for everyone." When both or all parties involved feel seen, heard, and understood, it becomes much easier to negotiate and problem-solve and find the best solutions that meet as many requirements as possible.

Before correcting, make a connection. It's easy for a parent to believe that they must either give in to their child's demands at the expense of other necessities (such as getting out the door) or become pushy. However, connecting before correcting works much better. Before facing what needs to happen, the parent may descend to the child's level, tune in to their environment, and build a connection. This frequently builds a bridge that allows the youngster to negotiate and provide a solution; "how about I just complete one more circuit on the track with my cars, and then I'll get dressed?" Keep in mind that children are far more cooperative in carrying out a strategy in which they play a role!

Chapter Nine
PARENTING THE ANXIOUS CHILD

Anxiety is a state of worry or fear that manifests as a combination of physical sensations, thoughts, and emotions.

Every kid and adolescent has anxiety at some point in their lives, and it is a natural part of growing up. They may experience anxiety at times, such as on their first day of school or before an exam, but they will soon calm down and feel better.

Anxiety can become a problem when a youngster feels trapped in it or overwhelming, upsetting, or uncontrollable. If this type of anxiety continues for an extended time, it can leave the child exhausted and isolated, limiting what they feel capable of doing.

If your child is suffering from anxiety, there are things you can do to help them, such as offering emotional support, working on practical solutions with them, and locating the appropriate professional treatment if they require it.

Depending on the individual, a child may experience anxiety for a multitude of reasons. Suppose your child is experiencing unmanageable levels of anxiety and fear. In that case, this is frequently an indication that something isn't quite right in their lives and that they require assistance in determining the source of the problem.

Some children and young people may get worried as a result of the following factors:

- undergoing a great deal of change in a short period of time, such as moving house or attending a new school
- having obligations beyond their age and development, such as caring for those in their

family

- being in the presence of someone who is extremely worried, such as a parent
- difficulties at school, such as feeling overwhelmed by work, tests, or peer groups
- suffering family stress around issues such as housing, money, and debt
- being bullied, watching or suffering abuse, or going through upsetting or traumatic circumstances in which they do not feel safe

Recognizing Anxiety Symptoms in Children

Children with anxiety may not show symptoms in the same manner as adults do. In addition to fear and stress, they may exhibit anger or irritation.

It's fair for parents to be concerned about their child's anxiety, but it's crucial to recognize that some juvenile anxiety is normal. Even so, some children do suffer from anxiety issues. Fortunately, there are things that parents can do to help their children in coping with anxiety or receiving treatment.

<u>Common childhood concerns</u>

A variety of things commonly induce concern and anxiety in children of various ages. New surroundings, demanding jobs, and even new people can cause fear and anxiety in youngsters at times.

Other age-appropriate apprehensions include:

- Stranger anxiety begins between the ages of 7 and 9 months and ends around the age of 30.
- Preschoolers' fear of the dark, monsters, insects, and animals
- Younger school-age children who are afraid of heights or storms
- Concerns about school and friends among older school-aged children and teenagers

These childhood worries are common and usually subside as a child grows older. It takes more than occasional anxiety, which is typical, to reveal true anxiety disorder symptoms.

<u>Anxiety signs and symptoms in children</u>

It is natural for children to experience anxiety occasionally, but it is also common to develop anxiety disorders. While prevalence estimates vary, the Centers for Disease Control and Prevention (CDC) estimates that about 7 percent of children aged 3 to 17 have diagnosable anxiety.

Children that have actual anxiety issues may suffer the following symptoms:

- Anger or aggression
- Trouble sleeping and nightmares

- Bedwetting
- Restlessness
- Getting in trouble at school
- Irritability
- Muscle tension
- Nervous habits such as nail-biting
- Avoiding certain situations
- Refusing to go to school
- Social withdrawal
- Low confidence and self-esteem
- Stomach aches
- Changes in appetite
- Headaches
- Trouble concentrating

Depending on the nature of the anxiety, the frequency and appearance of symptoms can vary. Some concerns (for example, social anxiety or phobia) may be triggered by specific circumstances, things, or places. Other types of anxiety, such as generalized anxiety disorder or panic disorder, can result in more frequent symptoms.

Other symptoms that interfere with a child's ability to learn, engage with classmates, sleep at night, or behave normally in daily life, are points of concern.

Typical childhood fears that remain past the age when they should dissipate (for example, being terrified of the dark or being apart from parents past the preschool age) are also cause for concern.

Dos and don'ts when children are anxious

When children are chronically worried, even the most well-meaning parents, who do not want their child to suffer, might exacerbate their anxiety. It occurs when parents want to protect their children from their concerns.

Here are some suggestions for helping children in breaking free from the cycle of anxiety.

<u>The goal is not to eradicate anxiety but rather to assist a child in managing it</u>

Nobody wants to see a child suffer, but the greatest way to assist children in overcoming anxiety isn't to try to eliminate the stressors that cause it. It is intended to assist them in learning to endure their anxiety and function as effectively as possible, even when they are nervous. As a result, the worry will lessen with time.

<u>Do not avoid situations simply because they make a child anxious</u>

Helping children avoid the things they are scared of may help them feel better in the short term, but it will exacerbate their anxiety in the long run. Assume a child in an unpleasant scenario becomes unhappy and begins to cry – not to be manipulative, but simply because that is how they feel. The youngster has acquired that coping method if their parents take them away or remove the object they're terrified of. This cycle has the potential to reoccur.

Communicate positive – yet reasonable – expectations

You can't promise a child that their concerns are unfounded—that they won't fail an exam, that they'll have a good time ice skating, or that another child won't make fun of them during show-and-tell. But you can show confidence that they'll be fine and will be able to handle it. You can also assure them that their anxiety level will decrease with time when they confront their fears. This provides them with trust that your expectations are reasonable and that you will not ask them to accomplish anything they are incapable of doing.

Respect their feelings, but don't give them authority

It is critical to remember that validation does not always imply agreement. So, if a child is scared of going to the doctor because they need a shot, you don't want to dismiss their anxieties, but you also don't want to exaggerate them. You want to listen and be empathic to them, help them understand why they're worried, and encourage them to believe they can overcome their worries. The message you want to convey is, "I realize you're terrified, and that's fine; I'm here to help you get through this."

Avoid asking leading questions

Encourage your child to express their emotions, but avoid asking leading questions such as, "Are you worried about the big test?" "Do you have any concerns about the science fair?" To avoid perpetuating the worry cycle, simply offer open-ended questions such as, "How do you feel about the science fair?"

Don't reinforce the child's worries

What you don't want to say with your tone of voice or body language is, "Perhaps this is something you should be terrified of." Assume a child has had a bad experience with a dog. You may be concerned about how they will react the next time they see a dog, and you may unwittingly transmit the message that they should be concerned.

Encourage the child to put up with their anxiety

Make it clear to your child that you recognize the effort it takes to withstand worry to complete what they want or need to do. It indeed encourages them to participate in life and let the anxiety follow its natural arc. It's referred to as the "habituation curve." That is, it will decrease over time as the child maintains contact with the stressor. It may not drop to zero or as quickly as you would wish, but it is how they can overcome their anxiety.

Try to keep the anticipating time as brief as possible

When we are terrified of something, the most challenging time is right before we do it. Another rule of thumb for parents is to remove or reduce the anticipation time as much as possible. If your child is anxious about going to a doctor's appointment, you don't want to start talking about it two hours before you go; this will likely make your child even more agitated. So just try to keep that time as brief as possible.

Discuss the situation with the child

It can be beneficial to discuss what would happen if a child's fear came true—how would they handle it? A youngster who is worried about being separated from their parents may be concerned about what would happen if a parent did not come to pick them up. As a result, we discuss it. What would you do if your mother did not arrive after soccer training? "Well, I'd tell the coach that my mother isn't here." What do you believe the coach would do? "Well, he'd call my mother, or he'd stay with me." A child worried that a stranger would be brought to pick them up can have their parents give them a code phrase that everyone who is sent will know. For some children, having a plan might help to reduce uncertainty healthily and productively.

Try to be an example of how to deal with anxiety healthily

You can assist children in dealing with anxiety in various ways by demonstrating how you manage it yourself. Kids are perceptive, and if you are constantly talking on the phone to a buddy about how you can't handle the stress or anxiety, they will pick up on it. I'm not saying you should pretend you don't experience worry and anxiety, but let your children hear or see you dealing with it calmly, accepting it, and feeling good about getting through it.

Chapter Ten
PARENTING THE STRONG-WILLED CHILD

What exactly is a strong-willed child? Some parents describe their children as "difficult," "stubborn," or, more favorably, "energetic." However, we might consider strong-willed children as persons of character who aren't easily moved from their points of view. Children with a strong will are lively and courageous. They like to study things for themselves rather than accept what others say;

therefore, they repeatedly push the boundaries. They passionately want to be "in charge" of themselves and will sometimes prioritize "being right" over everything else. When their hearts are set on something, their minds appear to have difficulty switching gears. Strong-willed children have great, passionate feelings and live life to the fullest.

Peaceful parenting your strong-willed child

Some parents believe that peaceful parenting is ineffective when dealing with a strong-willed child and that they require a more stringent approach. And yes, I am aware because many of the parents that approach me for assistance have a strong-willed child!! And believe me, when my strong-willed kid was younger, at times of absolute tiredness and frustration, I secretly had the same thinking! Sometimes, it felt like gently parenting such a strong-willed child was a social experiment gone wrong, and what if it backfired? There were definitely times when I wondered if injecting a little old-fashioned parent-induced dread might tame my child's wild spirit and put a stop to his gallop! I also have to say that when my heart was genuinely open to my brilliant, high-energy, passionate, fun-loving son, I winced at the prospect of ever having those thoughts. I'll go into more detail about my own experience with my strong-willed child later on.

In fact, there is no clean group or formula to which every strong-willed youngster can be assigned. Each child is unique, and each parent-child connection is complicated. Nonetheless, based on my own experience as a parent and as someone who has worked with families for decades, I am certain that peaceful parenting is especially crucial for children with strong personalities. Strong-willed youngsters are especially vulnerable to having very complex relationships with their parents, siblings, and themselves. They are especially vulnerable to being labeled tough and incurring the anger of teachers and family members.

Even though all children are emotionally sensitive and vulnerable, the strong-willed child can feel so deeply and passionately. Traditional authoritarian parenting styles can lead to a lot of unnecessary and heartbreaking conflict and power struggles for both parent and child. These children have a strong desire for some control over decisions that impact them and be treated fairly and respectfully. They need as much independence as they can handle safely, but they also need to feel held, guided and anchored.

When parents begin to practice a more calm, gentle parenting style, it may take some time to figure out how to maintain boundaries without imposing a punishment vs. reward system. There is frequently a difficult interval between opting not to employ penalties and learning or mastering new skills. As a result, the pendulum can swing back and forth between an authoritarian (parent's will overpowers the child's will) and a more permissive (child's will overpowers their parent's will) style, resulting in a great deal of instability and uncertainty. The dictatorial and permissive approaches do not provide the child with the skilled holding, guiding, and support that they require.

From giving orders to help our children

When parenting has been a challenge, parents may naturally be yearning for confirmation, or at least a glimmer of hope, that their increased patience and kindness are paying off! However, sometimes the youngster not only does not express thankfulness, but their protests become even louder!

Since the spirited child is less docile than a youngster with a different personality type, they usually attract a lot of pressure and hatred at home, kindergarten, school, and in their social group. According to research, employing an authoritarian approach with "alpha kids" is like throwing gasoline on the fire. They have frequently felt oppressed, weak, blamed, and misunderstood for acting in ways that appear to be beyond their control. And they've frequently lost faith in their parents' and teachers' belief in them. And if a parent or guardian loses faith in their child, how can they trust in themselves? We need this new peaceful parenting paradigm to guide these powerful, passionate, strong-willed little beings and allow them to share their incredible gifts with the rest of the world.

What does work in encouraging your strong-willed child to be the best version of themselves?

- Make it a priority to provide a safe environment for your sensitive, emotional child to communicate their actual ideas and feelings
- Laughter and play are key components of the puzzle! Especially power-reversal games in which the parent assumes the less powerful, less intelligent, and less aware position.
- Increase the amount of time you set aside for one-on-one interaction with your child.
- Commit to fully owning the anger and triggers that your strong-willed child instills in you, as well as modeling humility, effectively resolving confrontations, and restoring your child's dignity. They need to learn this stuff, you need to learn this stuff, and they won't figure it out unless you show them the way!
- Learn to keep the connection while imposing a restriction.
- The more good outlets kids have for all that huge energy (talking, moving, singing, playing, being in nature, etc.), the less likely they will turn to unhealthy outlets.

- As much as possible, use problem-solving instead of demands.
- Express more empathy than you may ever expect they require.

In an effort to prevent confrontations, parents can understandably become overly indulgent at times. However, while these children require some autonomy and should be involved in decision-making as much as possible, simply allowing them to do what they want, can leave them too much at the mercy of their intense desires and limited impulse control.

Remember that children require a lot of support in establishing self-discipline and self-control skills.

Chapter Eleven
MINDFULNESS IN PEACEFUL PARENTING

As parents, practicing mindfulness and modeling it for our children could be the component that shifts the balance from more chaos to increased happiness and harmony! Mindfulness is the deliberate slowing down and becoming present to our present experience, including our inner experience of thoughts, feelings, and sensations, with the purpose of witnessing without judgment or evaluation.

Mindful parenting

"But why is this significant for parents?" some may ask, "surely it's more pertinent to Buddhist monks sitting cross-legged in a temple with hours to kill!" Even while it may seem counter-intuitive to slow down and become consciously present when there is so much to accomplish, doing so can be the most beneficial thing we can do in our day! It is beneficial because the ability to see our inner and external experiences without judgment successfully reduces mental and emotional turbulence, gives comfort, and can thus move us out of the stress response and back to feeling calmer.

We can think, function, and feel so much better when we have exited the stress reaction (active sympathetic nervous system response)! Managing behavior in the family is primarily about managing stress, so the better we manage our own stress, the more tolerance we have to help our children manage theirs!

To most people, mindfulness is a wonderful idea linked with organics, yoga, and all that good stuff, but it's all very airy-fairy ethereal and difficult to understand why it's actually worth practicing. Even the term "practice" can be tiresome and seems the opposite of sitting in a hip cafe with coffee and cake, firing up those dopamine receptors! You might be thinking to yourself: Coffee and cake versus sitting with my muddled, stressed-out emotions!! Sure everyone would go for the first option, but let's clarify what mindfulness actually is, why it works, and what it can look like in your family.

What exactly is mindfulness?

Let me elaborate on the definition I provided above: Mindfulness is about purposefully slowing down and becoming present to our in-the-moment experience, including our inner experience of thoughts, feelings, and sensations, with the intention of witnessing without judgment or evaluation. What does it mean to slow down, become present to our experience, and witness without judgment, and why does it help?

Our thoughts grow more chaotic when we are agitated, and our breathing gets faster and shallower. Deciding to slow down and genuinely notice our reality is what mindfulness is all about. Mindfulness in action can be defined as resisting the impulse to keep doing and instead simply sitting with the aim to land and lower our tension. We pay close attention to our sitting experience, observing our thoughts and bodily sensations such as our chair contact and breathing.

Affirmations such as "I observe all these sensations" can totally help you in maintaining your thoughts on your current experience. This affirmation has stayed with me ever since I participated in a 10-day silent meditation program in a retreat some years ago. When we observe to accept rather than change, fixing or pushing away our thoughts, feelings, and sensations, we activate our witness consciousness, as it is known in some spiritual communities. Alternatively, we're applying the more logical perspective of our higher brain's thinking (the prefrontal cortex or upstairs brain) to the heightened emotions in the limbic and brain stem (or downstairs brain, as he calls it), which reduces mental and emotional chaos.

When a child is unable to sleep

When my son was younger, I would do this last activity with him if he couldn't sleep, and he'd fast go asleep. When he was a bit older, if he couldn't sleep, I'd tell him to "watch your breathing in your belly" and that I'd check on him shortly, and it always helped him fall asleep quickly. Any exercise that redirects our attention to our body awareness, whether as adults or children, provides better balance.

Bringing mindful parenting into daily life

On a hectic day, a parent picks up their child from kindy; an argument ensues when the youngster requests they go to the store for a treat; the debate continues until the parent recognizes their stress level has skyrocketed and knows they need to slow down and center themselves. Instead of continuing the debate, they focus their attention inward and check in to their breathing, noticing how strained it is. They now sense their body's urge to make each breath a little deeper and longer, taking in more air and totally releasing stress on their out-breath. They become aware of how their nerves react to their child's distress, they realize how tightly they hold their shoulders, neck, and jaws, and they instinctively drop their shoulders. They become aware of the blaming ideas flying through their heads, such as "just STOP child!", "Why do I fight back!" and "if their Dad didn't say yes to treats all the time!"

Witnessing their experience and relaxing their breathing decreases the pressure just enough to resist the impulse to raise their voice and instead say, "honey, it's not going to happen. I know this is difficult for you; let's do something nice together when we get home." The child may still be sad, but the parent can now begin to pay attention to their child's inner experience; "you're really disappointed, aren't you?"

The rapid respiration and stressful thoughts were signaling to the limbic emotional lower brain that there was a problem. Their emotional center was getting progressively overactive, hijacking the upper brain and making it difficult to think clearly. When stress levels rise, the right brain's imagination can run wild, connecting the dots to see all the contributing variables and imagining how things would worsen. "The entire day is destroyed, and it's going to be hard to achieve the deadline. No doubt hubby will be late again."

Stress reaction and brain training

Every time we choose to be aware, we practice focusing our minds and building our mental "muscles" in the same way we exercise our physical muscles. When confronted with actual threats, such as being physically attacked or being involved in a near-car accident, the stress response is acceptable and beneficial. The sympathetic nervous system response takes control. There is a massive rise in adrenalin and cortisol, giving us superhuman energy, strength, and speed and allowing our basic instincts of fight, flight, or freeze to take precedence over more systematic problems solving and strategy. In an emergency, this quick mobilization of energy across the body and brain is required.

That's all there is to it. Affirmations commonly used by those who teach and practice mindfulness include "it is that it is" and "I am that I am," both of which serve as reminders to accept our experience rather than reject, judge, or strive to escape it. Much peaceful parenting advice is based on these same principles. When we become truly present with our child and simply acknowledge their upset rather than reacting to it or attempting to fix it, our child can feel that presence; they may feel seen, heard, and cared for, which can be very soothing. Sometimes they scream louder because it seems safe to have that release, and sometimes they just slip in for an embrace, but these moments may be filled with amazing bonding.

Meditation impacts the mind! I've been practicing meditation for so long, and I've seen the results; it's truly the most potent healing agent anyone can introduce into their life. Suppose a parent managed to get up a little earlier that morning and do 15 minutes of meditation or sat in the garden listening to the birds with bare feet on the grass or even did a couple of yoga stretches. By doing so, they'll notice their stress level decreasing and their body much more relaxed. After all, it's the little things that add up to make a big difference.

CONCLUSION

It takes a lot of effort to be a peaceful parent. It's difficult to regulate ourselves when our child is misbehaving and pressing all of our buttons. With full lifestyles and busy schedules, it takes a lot of work to put energy into our connection with our children. It takes work to set limitations and develop strategies to scaffold and assist our child. And it requires fortitude to go against the grain of our society and teach our children without using punishment.

This method is not permissive, and it does not allow children to do whatever they want because children require limitations and parental guidance. However, calm parenting differs from traditional parenting. Traditional parenting believes that the best method to stop or change a child's undesirable conduct is to either ignore it or respond with punishment, threats, or bribery. In contrast, peaceful parenting argues that children behave in irritating, challenging, and disagreeable ways for a variety of reasons other than being "bad."

First, children's brains are not fully matured, and their impulse control is still limited. Second, kids are overwhelmed by their enormous emotions, and they "act out" sentiments they can't handle. So, if we wish to eliminate the actions that irritate us (such as kicking, biting, throwing items, hurting siblings, and so on), we must go to the source of the problem, which involves helping our children with their huge feelings. When parents can support their children in managing their emotions, they can better manage their behavior.

It takes effort and commitment to transition to peaceful parenting, and it is an investment in yourself, your child, and your family.

But it's well worth it if we want kind, responsible, independent, and resilient children who care about what we think and want to spend time with us as they grow up.

About Author

In 2006, Nora Willams began her career in therapy by assisting individuals, families, and couples in rebuilding their lives and relationships after facing life's challenges. As a therapist, Nora Williams works with people to uncover their desires and empower them to make positive changes in their life. She recognizes that seeking help can be challenging, so she uses a non-judgmental approach to help people feel supported in their counseling journey.

www.ingramcontent.com/pod-product-compliance
Lightning Source LLC
Chambersburg PA
CBHW070106120526
44588CB00032B/1264